HR WITHOUT PEOPLE?

The Future of Work

The future of work is a vital contemporary area of debate both in business and management research, and in wider social, political and economic discourse. Globally relevant issues, including the ageing workforce, rise of the gig economy, workplace automation and changing forms of business ownership, are all regularly the subject of discussion in both academic research and the mainstream media, having wider professional and public policy implications.

The Future of Work series features books examining key issues or challenges in the modern workplace, synthesising prior developments in critical thinking, alongside current practical challenges in order to interrogate possible future developments in the world of work.

Offering future research agendas and suggesting practical outcomes for today's and tomorrow's businesses and workforce, the books in this series present powerful, challenging and polemical analysis of a diverse range of subjects in their potential to address future challenges and possible new trajectories.

The series highlights what changes still need to be made to core areas of business practice and theory in order for them to be forward facing, more representative and able to fulfill the industrial challenges of the future.

OTHER TITLES IN THE SERIES

Algorithms, Blockchain and Cryptocurrency: Implications for the Future of the Workplace
Gavin Brown and Richard Whittle

FORTHCOMING TITLES

The Healthy Workforce: Enhancing Wellbeing and Productivity in the Workers of the Future
Stephen Bevan and Cary L. Cooper

Spending Without Thinking: The Future of Consumption
Richard Whittle

The Future of Recruitment: Using the new science of talent analytics to get your hiring right
Tomas Chamorro-Premuzic, Franziska Leutner and Reece Akhtar

Cooperatives at Work
George Cheney, Matt Noyes and Emi Do

HR WITHOUT PEOPLE?

Industrial Evolution in the Age of Automation, AI, and Machine Learning

BY

ANTHONY R. WHEELER
Widener University, USA

And

M. RONALD BUCKLEY
University of Oklahoma, USA

emerald
PUBLISHING

United Kingdom – North America – Japan – India
Malaysia – China

Emerald Publishing Limited
Howard House, Wagon Lane, Bingley BD16 1WA, UK

First edition 2021

British Library Cataloguing in Publication Data
A catalogue record for this book is available from the British Library

ISBN: 978-1-80117-040-6 (Print)
ISBN: 978-1-80117-037-6 (Online)
ISBN: 978-1-80117-039-0 (Epub)

ISOQAR certified
Management System,
awarded to Emerald
for adherence to
Environmental
standard
ISO 14001:2004.

Certificate Number 1985
ISO 14001

INVESTOR IN PEOPLE

To my co-author, who has made a greater impact on my life than any other mentor
                                                        - Anthony R. Wheeler

To Marsha, Kathleen, and Christopher
                                                        - M. Ronald Buckley

CONTENTS

ABOUT THE AUTHORS

Anthony R. Wheeler is the Dean of the School of Business Administration and a Professor of Management at Widener University. His research focuses on employee turnover and retention, employee stress, burnout, engagement, and leadership. He has published in *Journal of Management, Journal of Applied Psychology, Journal of Organizational Behavior, Journal of Business Research, Work & Stress, Leadership Quarterly, Journal of Occupational and Health Psychology, International Journal of Selection and Assessment, Journal of Business Ethics,* and *Journal of Business Logistics.* He is a co-editor of *Research in Personnel and Human Resources Management* and has consulted for Fortune 500 companies, start-ups, and governments.

M. Ronald Buckley holds the JC Penney Company Chair of Business Leadership and is a Professor of Management and a Professor of Psychology in the Michael F. Price College of Business at the University of Oklahoma. He earned his PhD in I-O Psychology from Auburn University. He is interested in many topics in Human Resources Management, e.g., interview decision-making, fairness and bias in selection, and organizational socialization. Buckley has written over 160 peer-reviewed articles, many of which have appeared in the *Journal of Management, Academy of Management Review,*

Journal of Applied Psychology, Personnel Psychology, Educational and Psychological Measurement, Leadership Quarterly, Organizational Behavior and Human Decision Processes, and the *Journal of Organizational Behavior.*

PREFACE

Depending on the movie or book, the natural end point of artificial intelligence and machine learning is either the destruction of humankind at the hands of the machines or the general atrophy of the human body, mind, and spirit such that our bleary-eyed existence will be reduced to machine-assisted movement and a technology-enabled continuous stream of audio-visual entertainment to keep our brains occupied during waking hours. With the Internet of Things (IoT) linking every device, appliance, and machine, perhaps one day a self-aware network of appliances will conspire to rid their world of human threats while we do our laundry or reach for a cold beverage in our refrigerator – a scene ripped from *The Terminator* itself. Perhaps one day, humans will lounge all day in motorized personal chairs that carry us from our beds to breakfast to morning movie time to lunch and so forth such that we evolve into pure *id* biological masses that no longer resemble our now-distant *Homo sapiens* relatives – something the Disney-Pixar film *WALL-E* portrays. Or perhaps humans adapt and evolve to use technological advances to spur a new age of Renaissance where our creativity leads to breathtaking advancements in art, music, and literature that makes us more human than we have ever been.

Getting from where automation, artificial intelligence, and machine learning currently exists to whatever future might exist for humans and machines will not be a simple straight-line narrative. How humans and machines evolve will change nearly every facet of human existence, including how we work – and the meaning of that work – and how work influences almost every organizing structure in the world today – companies, industries, government, societies. That span of organizing structures through the lens of human resources management is the purpose of this book. That is, automation, artificial intelligence, and machine learning will change how humans think about the role of work in their lives and how organizations – the force driving automation, artificial intelligence, and machine learning – will use their human resources management systems to influence the meaning of work, the role of jobs, and the sense of belonging that all humans derive from their work. This is the seminal reciprocal relationship between humans and work.

Yet these trends are not new. Societies became aware of automation during and in the aftermath of War Wars 1 and 2. During the 1980s, car manufacturers began to embrace the use of machines to automate portions of vehicle production. An IBM machine – dubbed Deep Blue – famously defeated world chess champion Gary Kasparov in 1997, signaling an advancement in artificial intelligence. At the turn of the twenty-first century, many economically advanced nations had entered into the *Knowledge Economy* where generating ideas and services created significantly more economic value than did making things. Terms like "human capital" emerged amid the *Knowledge Economy*, meaning that companies could leverage the cumulative knowledge, skills, and abilities of their employees to create, nurture, and sustain competitive advantages in their markets. In the *Knowledge Economy*, people mattered. Companies quickly realized that the old stereotype of human resources management as a back office, pushing papers, and only adding to a company's overhead costs did not mesh with a globally competitive business environment. As outsourcing to lower labor cost countries became more expensive and was paired with advances in robotics, artificial intelligence, and machine learning, human capital disruption in labor markets – people – became inescapable. This is the inevitable result of the *Knowledge Economy* ceding to the reality of what some have called the "Fourth Industrial Revolution" – one that is based on automation, artificial intelligence, and machine learning.

Meanwhile, secondary, vocational or technical, and higher education have tried to keep pace with preparing students to enter a workforce that looks remarkably different from the workforce that their parents entered. Science, technology, engineering, and math – STEM – programs at the secondary/high school level have sprouted up all over the world, teaching children at younger ages new technological advances and applications. Vocational or technical training programs have heavily focused on computer and technology-based courses. Automotive mechanics work as much now with computer terminals as they do with wrenches. In higher education, "analytics" now pervades general education requirements at colleges and universities. Formerly art-based majors like graphic design now minor or double-major in marketing. Accounting programs regularly include analytics courses instead of additional tax or auditing courses.

In the United States alone, college and universities enroll over 250,000 accounting majors per year and graduate just under 80,000 students per year with bachelor and master degrees. This supply of students feeds 42,000 accounting firms, who combined employ 1.3 million accountants. An additional 300,00 certified public accountants (CPAs) work inside of corporations as opposed to public accounting firms. These figures do not include people in the workforce who do not hold CPAs or even accounting degrees but work in accounting-related jobs like bookkeepers, payroll clerks, corporate financial analysts, staff accountants, or accountants working with non-profits or all levels of government. The broadest estimate in the United States of the number of people working within the field of accounting nears 11 million people.[1] Globally, that number soars by multiple factors.

Over the past decade, accounting firms across the globe have invested billions of dollars into automation, artificial intelligence, and machine learning technologies. While firms might have in the past outsourced entry-level tasks to low-cost overseas partners, the economics of outsourcing increasingly yield smaller cost savings when compared to what an algorithm or bot can accomplish with greater volume. Outsourcing labor still provides cost-competitive advantages in some industries, but in the accounting industry, it appears that outsourcing does not provide the same advantages. Advances in data analytics, computing power and data storage, and analytic technical skills of talented data scientists have created disruption in the field of accounting.

Over the next 20 years, 40% of basic accounting jobs will be automated. Technologies like blockchain, which automatically leaves an audit trail, change how auditing functions within firms and companies will operate. On the audit side, estimates suggest that fewer than 100 firms in the United States will be needed to handle all of the auditing work that is now done by thousands of firms.[2] Add in that many companies – some estimates suggest over 30%[3] – plan to outsource their financial functions, which includes mostly entry-level accounting job duties, within their units, and the field of accounting looks likely to significantly contract over the coming decades. At the macro level, this means that millions of accounting jobs within the US workforce will be displaced over a relatively short period of time. A classic supply and demand mismatch warily looms on the horizon. Institutions of higher education produce thousands of graduates that head out into an industry known for high paying jobs and long careers as that industry morphs into a smaller, more analytic, more technologically driven industry. The accounting industry will be alive and financially well in the *Fourth Industrial Revolution*, but it will likely not employ nearly as many people as it now does.

These effects, of course, are not limited to the accounting industry. Artificial automation, intelligence, and machine learning will impact numerous industries. Across the entire US workforce, for instance, up to 73 million jobs – a full third of the US workforce – could be displaced by automation, artificial intelligence, and machine learning in the next 10 years.[4] Unlike previous industrial revolutions, the *Fourth Industrial Revolution* might not create new industries and jobs to replace those who are displaced. The question that this book tries to answer, in everyday business and not academic terms, is, how will the business field of human resources management – the people function – respond to these paradigm shifting changes and potential realities? We start by examining the importance of work for humans and societies that artificial intelligence, machine learning, and automation actively gainsay. We then explore how human resources management functions within businesses will adapt in the near-, mid-, and long term. Finally, we peer into a future of smaller full-time workforces where human resources management can be leveraged to potentially usher in a new Renaissance and what that might mean for people and societies. Obviously, no one can predict the future with exact certitude, but patterns and trends can be extrapolated. So, what happens to human resources management when there are no or fewer jobs? Let us start with the beginning and hopefully begin a discussion.

1

THE EVOLUTION OF HUMANS AND THEIR WORK

Take a moment to think about who you are as a person. After saying your name, how do you describe yourself to others upon first introduction? Do you begin your description with a set of nouns that convey a set of relationships – are you a mother or father? Do you begin your description with a location – where are you from? Do you begin your description with words about belonging to groups, teams, or organizations – are you with these people; do you work for this company? Or do you often introduce yourself based upon what you do for work – are you a human resources management professional? Obviously, situations dictate to a certain extent how you will initially describe yourself, but chances are that you will refer to your work or for whom and with who you work when describing who you are as a person. Whether you like your work or your employer very much or not, your work is fundamental to who you are as a person. Our work not only gives us a sense of self and expression but also provides us with opportunities – opportunities to move, opportunities

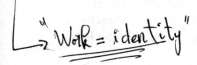

1

to provide, opportunities for fulfillment, opportunities of relationships and love, opportunities of freedom. Or work can, similarly, restrict all of those opportunities.

Some might argue that work provides nothing more than a means to an end. With work comes money or remuneration. With money comes the ability to purchase goods or services that sustain life, such as food, shelter, and safety. With money comes the ability to live a life of status or esteem. That is, some argue that the money earned through work can satisfy both our needs and wants. However, work – one's own work – can be dissociated from money. Consider that some people never work a day in their lives for need of money because they have wealth from previous generations. Yet even those who have inherited wealth often choose to work or assume a vocation – derived from Latin to mean "a calling" – to not just occupy their time but also to find some sort of meaning in their lives.

Moreover, money itself holds differential meaning for people and even societies.[1] Before the advent of money, people engaged in barter – an exchange between goods or services that required a time-consuming and sometimes messy process of establishing comparative worth between exchanged goods or services – that rendered money largely irrelevant in most societies. Money, however, and the meaning ascribed to is still relative. In more individualistic societies, money increases the focus on personal goal attainment while money erodes communal behaviors in more collectivist societies. Simply stated, money disrupts cohesion and harmony between, with, and among people. People also vary in their attitudes toward money and the value they ascribe to money in terms of whether or not money is needed to live one's life the way one chooses to live that life. Inside of organizations, money is a known disruptor due to perceptions of equity or fairness in terms of how the organization distributes money in exchange for work. An employee can find perfect contentment in his or her salary, which satisfies both that person's wants and needs. Yet when that employee learns that a coworker earns more money – for doing the same job or another job altogether – that employee will suddenly feel dissatisfaction with the employer, become frustrated with how the employer treats employees, and likely begin looking for a new job in another company. The simple knowledge that a coworker earns more money can radically alter not only how one views his or her employer but also how one assesses how much money is now needed to cover his or her wants and needs. To further demonstrate the relativity of money, try the following experiment. In your mind, think about how much money you need to earn to happily live your life. Put an actual figure on that amount of money. Now ask your friends, family members, and coworkers that same question and ask if they will tell you their figures. What you will likely find is that your monetary figure will increase upon hearing what others' monetary needs to live a happy life are.

Not that people naturally talk about their earnings in social settings. Typically, the work one does will convey the social meaning of affluence or status. More to the point, though, is that people seldom describe themselves in terms of how much money they make. Money might provide the means to whatever ends a person wants or needs, but money does not provide the sense of self or belonging that one's job provides.

It is important to understand the pairing of "sense of self and belonging" mentioned above, as it helps to further explain why work becomes integral to one's sense of self. Humans by nature and evolution are primarily social animals, something obfuscated by pop – and quite frankly, junk – psychology that virally spreads through social media and the Internet. Even an introvert, someone whose natural predisposition is to prefer one-on-one or small group conversations as opposed to the extrovert's predisposition to prefer large group settings, is a social creature.

Work = "Sense of self & belonging"

Humans have a primary motivation to belong to groups that they feel are attractive and important. Belonging to a personally attractive group reflects favorably onto the individual. If a person belongs to an attractive group, it must mean that the individual is an important or good or attractive individual. This explains why companies with high brand identity receive not just more applicants for job openings but also significantly better applicants. Working for a highly recognizable company boosts the self-esteem of the employees who work for that company. It says something about who you are as a person to work for such a well-known and esteemed company.

Delving deeper into the psychological power of belonging to groups and how belonging to those groups alters your sense of self, consider what occurs to individuals when the groups they belong to come under attack or scrutiny. Let us assume you proudly work for a company that you feel is considered an industry leader. Your LinkedIn and other social media profiles display your work affiliation. You own company-branded apparel that you wear outside of work. Your company is a good company, and you are a good person. Unrelated to your actual job or even division, a public scandal hits your company. Word leaks and spreads quickly through the Internet and news media. Instead of reading or hearing about how great your company is, you now only hear negative things about your company. How do you feel about this? Do you proudly wear your company-branded apparel outside of work? Do you shy away from discussions about work with friends and family? You likely feel cognitive dissonance – you are a good person but you work for a scandalous company. You will feel the need to alleviate this dissonance. Will you leave the company? Or will you double-down on your affiliation with the company? It is still a good company that employed people who did wrong, but that does not mean the entire company is bad. It does not mean you are bad.

This type of process plays out every day in almost every facet of one's life. This social identity process explains why groups of people have fought wars against each other for reasons that in hindsight appear trivial. Yet, when one's group is attacked – even verbally – it feels as though you as an individual are attacked. In defending your group's honor, status, or physical well-being, you are in fact defending your honor, status, and well-being. The levels of this social identity process can scale from a small unit of a group or team to a company to an industry or profession to a society. We see this social identity process play out in rivalries between sports teams, which can lead to physical violence among followers. We see this social identity process play out in labor relations settings. We see this social identity process play out in national politics, as political polarization continues to spread across the globe.

In terms of work, humans often identify with what they do for work, with companies and industries to which they belong, and with the professions to which they belong. It starts with what we do and scales to larger groups as societies scale in complexity. Consider surnames that provide hereditary links to previous generations. The English surname Wright derives from wood working. The surname Fletcher derives from the French word for arrows used by archers. The Italian surname Bagni derives from someone who worked as a bathhouse attendant. The Spanish surname Cervantes derives from those who worked as servants. The Greek surname Bakirtzis derives from coppersmiths. The German surname Farber denotes someone who worked as a dyer. The Chinese surname Zhang is believed to have derived from bowmakers. All of these examples demonstrate how powerful the connection is between work and an individual's identity. It is so strong that for some people, their work is their name. Your family may have been one that constructed wheels (Wheeler) or were primarily herdsmen (Buckley).

Identifying people based on they work they do or the profession they belong to dates to the Middle Ages. During this feudal time period before the age of enlightenment, work was largely based around serving the needs, wants, and operation of a local royal's kingdom or principality. The local royal owned the lands, resources, and means of production of all people living in that kingdom or principality. An array of skilled trade jobs and professions proliferated in feudal economic systems: multiple types of smiths working with different metals to produce products or military armament, tanners and cobblers working with animal hides to produce garments and shoes, masons and carpenters working with materials to build structures, millers and bakers taking farmed grains and creating bread, and falconers and grooms working with animals. What one did for his or her work on behalf of the royalty was passed down from generation to generation, often through heredity and an apprenticeship vocational training system, and guilds to protect and oversee trades. If your father farmed the land to provide food for the royal's kingdom or principality, his surname – perhaps Farmer – would denote that occupation. The farmer's offspring inherited that surname and likely worked the land for generations to come. As the Enlightenment, Renaissance, and Industrial Revolution came, the work or profession of one's offspring might change, but the surnames continued to pass from generation to generation.

During the Middle Ages and clear through the Enlightenment, Renaissance, and Industrial Revolution, Western religions reinforced the link between work and one's self.[2] Protestant denominations interpreted parts of the Bible as meaning that one's work on Earth could lead to salvation in the afterlife. The phrase *Protestant Work Ethic* captures this linkage between work and one described self, albeit through the mechanism of religion. In order to be "saved" by their god, one must work hard in his or her daily life. Hard work became a way to demonstrate that one is a good person. Work literally fused to an individual's identity and salvation to the afterlife.

This leads to the question, though, of the identification of work to one's self being a recent evolutionary outcome. In the recent history – roughly 200,000 years – of human biological and social evolution, did humans begin to identify work with their sense of self only over the past 1,000 years? Anthropological research points to a longer period of time. The evolutionary ancestors of modern humans – *Homo erectus* – began organizing in hunting and gathering groups, likely family-sized units, more than 1.8 million years ago.[3] Instead of a nomadic lifestyle that followed migratory patterns of food sources and seasonal weather patterns that affected both animals and plants, some hunting and gathering societies migrated to areas where resources could be hunted and gathered in a single geographic area. Specialized tools and hunting and gathering techniques were created to sustainably develop and exploit this type of environment Modern humans – *Homo sapiens* – specifically evolved as hunters and gatherers and refined the hunting and agriculture techniques that allowed for the development of larger, more complex societies. However, even in these older human societies, the roles of hunting or fishing and gathering or farming were divided among people – largely based on biological sex – within the family units or societies. Men tended to be the hunters, while women tended to be the gatherers. In these ancient family structures and societies, what one did – hunting or gathering – was part of who they were.

We see the multiple factors that embed and reinforce work as central to one's identity. Evolutionary, social, familial, and religious forces have shaped the centrality of work to humans. Several outcomes, of course, occur as a result of the

centrality of work to humans and an individual's identity.
This gets to the heart of the meaning of work for anyone.
How anyone describes themselves is complex, as any individual has a complex self. We occupy many roles in our lives.
We have myriad interests and hobbies. We maintain dozens
of relationships; some close and some distant. Some of these
roles, interests, and relationships are more or less salient to
us at any given point in time. Based on circumstances –
perhaps a wedding or a funeral – your role as parent or
sibling can become more important or active in how you
describe yourself. Yet that active role can become less
important as circumstances change. Perhaps when sitting in
the stands and cheering as your favorite football team battles
its primary rival in a crosstown derby, your identity as a
parent or sibling matters very little at that time. What is
important to understand about the saliency of roles, interests, and relationships to one's self is that not only are these
roles, interests, and relationships associated with positive
feelings and emotions, but also that the more roles, interests,
and relationships that one identifies with, the more one is
open to having parts of one's self exposed to potentially
negative outcomes. That is, the more the things you identify
with, the more those things are open to being threatened or
attacked. Recall that humans derive their identities, in part,
through groups with which they identify. Those associations
make us feel good about who we are. If an association is
threatened or attacked by an outsider to that association, the
attack is personal as if it happened to us. Now think about
multiple roles, interests, and relationships in that regard. The
more we identify with, the more we are exposed to potential
identity threats.

Fortunately, humans have adapted to cope with the
complexities of how we self-identify and threats to self-
identity. Back to the point of saliency, some roles, interests,

and relationships occupy more central places in how we describe ourselves, while others become more peripheral to ourselves. Not that these peripheral aspects of ourselves cannot become more active based on circumstances – think about attending that derby – but those peripheral aspects of our lives are likely more compartmentalized than the primary aspect of ourselves. When your favorite team loses the derby against its crosstown rival, you might feel upset for a brief amount of time; but there is always the next game or the next year. However, for those central aspects of ourselves, experiencing an attack, threat, or actual loss of those aspects of ourselves can be devastating to our overall sense of self. A death, a break-up of a marriage or partnership, or the loss of a job have been known to send even the strongest of people into a spiral that can last long periods of time and spread into other parts of one's self.

Aside from the evolution, social, familial, and religious factors that embed and reinforce work as a central part of one's identity, think more concretely about the role that work plays in your life. For most adults, as previously discussed, work provides opportunities to satisfy needs and wants. Work also occupies a large amount of time in anyone's daily life. You might only technically work a nine-hour day, but you likely take work home with you in some form or fashion. You likely check and respond to your work email and phone messages after work hours. You likely plan your next work day activities – maybe even something as trivial as what you plan to wear to work the next day – after work hours. If you are able to take a vacation or holiday, you likely spend the early and late parts of those work breaks thinking about work issues – what you are leaving and what you will return to. Outside of familial or close personal relationships, your work is central to not just your daily life but also to who you are as a person.

An entire field of academic and practitioner study explores the boundaries between your work and the other parts of your life. The boundary between work and home or family is relatively permeable. That is, few people can entirely compartmentalize work and home or family. When a negative event occurs at your job, you likely have difficulty containing the negative spillover to just your work. Similarly, when something negative occurs in your home or family life, you likely have difficulty containing the negativity to just your home or family life. Yes, sometimes work or home or family can act as a respite or getaway to events occurring in the other aspects of your life, but, generally speaking, your work and home or family lives often and easily spillover into the other domains of your life. When spillover does occur, either positive or negative, it affects both domains. Divorce has been known to affect work to the point where job change or loss occurs. Alternatively, work stress often follows an employee home. Burnout – the psychological state of emotional exhaustion, withdrawal, and reduced self-efficacy – has been known to significantly disrupt home and family relationships. All of this again speaks to the centrality of work to who we are as humans.

The meaning work provides you is more than just how happy you are at work with what you do or how your company treats you. It is true that job satisfaction and organizational commitment strongly predict whether or not you will choose to remain or leave your employer.[4] Work can provide a sense of fulfillment to someone. Accomplishing work and career goals makes one feel not only elated in the short term but also pride in the long term. Work also can provide a creative outlet for humans. While many might associate creativity with the arts, creativity and the application of creativity to useful and implementable ends – known as innovation – occurs in all facets of one's life. Solving a challenging problem at work requires creativity. Developing new ideas, processes, and products requires creativity and innovation. As we solve problems and create new ideas, processes, and products, we experience joy. It makes us feel better about who we are as people, not just in a domain or job function-specific way that self-efficacy describes but also in a global sense of how happy we are with ourselves – what we know as self-esteem. The joy we feel and the positive state of mind that it creates then makes us potentially more creative. That is, a virtuous, reinforcing progression forms where our creativity creates job and positive affect, which opens and expands our thinking so that we become more creative.[5] From this perspective, work-enabled problem-solving, creativity, and innovation provide the fuel for entrepreneurship and new venture creation. That is, the meaningfulness we experience through work ultimately leads to larger societal structures that provide social and material resources to others in a society.

If work provides a sense of self, enables rich social interactions, provides opportunities to fulfill needs and wants, fuels creativity and innovation, and is deeply ingrained in the human experience through evolution and even religion, what happens when work potentially goes away? We might already have a sense of what it can do to individuals, as people do not work forever and retire from their jobs and careers. Removing work from one's life leads to increases in physical and mental health troubles, including increased reports of malaise and depression.[6]

Predictably, the loss of work makes one feel less positive about one's self. As previously discussed, the feeling of loss, or even the threat of loss, of one of the core dimensions of a person's self can be distressing. The threat of loss explains why someone might feel apprehension about retiring, and that apprehension will have the same effect on one's overall well-being as does the actual loss of part of one's core self-dimensions.

Loss or the threat of loss of what one values – from material resources to emotional resources to status or esteem resources – creates stress. When that stress is unmitigated, it leads to emotional exhaustion, depersonalization or withdrawal, and reduced self-efficacy and performance. These are the core dimensions of burnout. At the extreme end of burnout are issues like depression. Chronic burnout has been linked to ruinous health outcomes – weight gain, heart attack, pneumonia, self-harm – as well as the destruction of social relationships. So, this is the paradox facing retirees and likely larger segments of a workforce that gets displaced by automation, artificial intelligence, and machine learning: As one depersonalizes and withdraws from relationships, it is the social relationships that will buffer the effects of burnout. Moreover, as previously mentioned, one's sense of self can expand or collapse based upon situations. The expansion of self-categorizations can not only leave one's self open to more threats but can also have a beneficial effect. The broader one's self-concept, the lesser any single dimension can affect one's overall well-being. So, yet here is another paradox for a retiree or displaced workers: emotional exhaustion makes it difficult to muster the energy to take on the new roles that expand one's self. Further, burnout robs individuals of their belief that they can perform tasks or be successful in things that they were once quite successful in doing. That lack of self-efficacy can spread to other areas of one's life, which can lead to depression. Just when someone needs to take on new roles, they question whether or not they can successfully take on new roles. For retirees, they can fill in or expand the other domains of their self to compensate for the loss of work and the meaning it provides to one's self. Relying on close or familial relationships, volunteering for a beloved cause or charity, and even continuing to work on a limited or part-time basis can limit the loss of self that is tied to work.

In a world of automation, artificial intelligence, and machine learning displacing workers in multiple industries, this process can play out over a much longer timeframe. Again, using retirement as a proxy, consider in the United States that over 100,000 people retire each month.[7] More than 1 million Americans each year go through the process of adjusting to the loss of a core dimension of their self, which in a nation of 330 million people might not raise too many alarms. Let us return, however, to the example of the accounting industry from the preface of this book. An industry employing more than 10 million people will likely rapidly contract over the next decade, shedding millions of jobs that employ people far younger than retirement age. As the threat of job loss increases due to automation, artificial intelligence, and machine learning increases, those employees will begin to feel stress that can lead to burnout. As the actual workforce contraction begins, the stress–burnout cycle will only strengthen. When you apply this across multiple established and well-paid jobs and industries, the outlines of a public mental and physical health crisis emerge.

What starts with an individual – the meaning of work in one's life – coupled with a rapidly changing job market and career expectancy will predictably scale into problems for larger social structures. You might be thinking right now, "I've heard this before with jobs going away and never coming back, but new industries and jobs always replace the old one." Yes, that might again be the case for the *Fourth Industrial Revolution*. In some ways, that might be beside the point. The change has already started, it has started to displace jobs in specific industries, and people currently must deal with the loss of their sense of self that is related to their work. This is already occurring now in many economically advanced nations. Until those new industries and jobs emerge, millions of people worldwide currently experience the economic displacement of the *Fourth Industrial Revolution*, which personally might as well be considered the displacement of one's sense of self. We should not underestimate the in-progress impact of removing a core component of the human experience – one that has developed over hundreds of thousands of years – not just to people but also to societies.

2

THE IMPORTANCE OF WORK TO SOCIETIES

Perhaps a civilization can end and be absorbed into another civilization without a final cataclysmic military battle or war being waged. Perhaps an entire civilization can assimilate into another because of economics. Roughly a thousand years before the Common Era on the Italian Peninsula, a civilization – the Etruscan civilization – spanned from the middle of the peninsula to the Alps. At its peak, the Etruscan civilization rivaled and sometimes eclipsed the Roman civilization that grew to dominate the Mediterranean region and through what is now Western Europe. The Etruscans surely engaged in armed conflict with other regional civilizations vying for control of the Italian peninsula and beyond. From roughly 900 BCE to the early 300s BCE, the Etruscans, Carthaginians, and ascendant Rome fought for supremacy of the region. Yet as the Hellenic period of Rome rise to becoming an empire as Greece's Mediterranean empire receded, the Etruscan civilization continued to exist – through an alliance of 12 fortified hill cities in central Italy – as Rome controlled the entire Italian peninsula. The last battle fought between the Romans and

Etruscans occurred in 264 BCE, but the Etruscan civilization is believed to have survived, surrounded by Rome, until 27 BCE How did the Etruscan civilization end without a bang? It appears as the Etruscans ensconced themselves in their fortified hill cities, the Romans engaged commerce in the valleys and towns surrounding the Etruscan cities. As the Etruscans did business with the Romans, they slowly assimilated – culturally and politically – into greater Rome.

Of course, it helped that Rome had the most powerful army in the known world protecting its commercial interests, but the history of the Etruscans shows how commerce can smoothly result in the absorption and assimilation of societies. If the meaning of work is crucial to the identity of humans, the outcomes of human work play a commensurately large role in shaping human societies and civilizations. The human activity of work plays an organizing role in the development of societies. Groups of people working toward a common goal of producing specific products or services form businesses. Governing organizations levy taxes on individual incomes and businesses. Government provides public services for the greater good of its citizens – education, social programs, infrastructure, defense, and the like. Individual work ties personages together into larger groups of people, which thusly support larger social structures like towns, cities, states, and nations. Behind every empire sits an economic power – from Rome to England to the United States to the emerging China.

Adam Smith's *An Inquiry into the Nature and Causes of the Wealth of Nations* tied a direct line between the work of humans to the creation of business and wealth and the rise of cities as industrial centers to national political structures that govern economies and societies. In Smith's philosophizing, the creation of manufacturing allowed for greater production of goods compared to agrarian jobs and societies. Money replaced bartering. Those with wealth had the means and resources to control the production of goods, which created a division of labor between workers and owners. The demand from markets for specific good facilitates the creation of those goods, which also influences the growth of businesses that fulfill the supply of those goods to the markets. Businesses grow by adding capacity and employees, who receive remuneration for their work efforts. Political systems develop to govern these processes and relationships. National economies grow and contract along the supply and demand contours of the goods and services that nations create and provide to their populations or the populations of other nations. If you have a flashback to your micro- and macroeconomics courses as a student, it is understandable.

All of this economic activity takes place in a broad context, however, that is important to understand. Nations possess cultures that describe the values, beliefs, and norms of behaviors that are expected of citizens living in those nations. Whether you ascribe to Hofstede's national culture dimensions or that of the GLOBE study, nations vary in their cultures, which shapes the relationships between people, their work, their fellow citizens, and their government. In collective national cultures, the good of the group is valued over the good of the individual. In masculine national cultures, roles within a country are ascribed by traditional gender roles. In nations with low power distance, the top and the bottom of society have little differentiation. So, in a collective culture like in Japan, an individual's work accomplishments pale in comparison to a team's work accomplishments. In a masculine culture like in Mexico, men typically work in professions that adhere to traditional male roles in that nation. In a low power distance nation like Sweden, wealthy and less wealthy citizens are largely treated the same. National culture not just describes what citizens value and believe or how citizens will treat each other but also informs the legal systems that nations construct to codify the values, beliefs, and norms of behaviors for individuals and countries.

Beginning with the smallest unit of work that leads to the development of business and economic activity, entrepreneurs are synonymous with their work and businesses. Many countries tout entrepreneurship as the foundation of their economies. When you think of entrepreneurs today, you might think of people like Elon Musk, Richard Branson, Sergey Brin, Mark Zuckerberg, Ophrah Winfrey, Steve Jobs, or Martha Stewart. In each of these examples, you likely associate a company or business activity with these successful entrepreneurs. Each had an innovative idea, started a business, and grew that business into a lucrative global enterprise. In many cases, each entrepreneur listed above has the brand of their company fused to their name. Their work, their passion, their company, their success, or their celebrity is tied to their name and who they are as people. Local and national governments use a host of incentives – tax breaks, direct investment, incubators, and accelerators – to spur innovation and support new venture creation. The work of a single entrepreneur can create thousands of jobs that benefit societies, whether through creating new work opportunities for citizens or by expanding the tax base to support government social programs.

Perhaps one level of analysis up from entrepreneurs are family business, which have been estimated to generate between 70 and 90% of the world's gross domestic product.[1] Whether a family restaurant or a convenience store or an accounting or law practice, family businesses are typically much smaller and employ far fewer people than what we think of when thinking about a company. This is not to say that family business cannot grow to quite large entities. The Wahaha Group in China has grown from a small single-item beverage company to a multinational company with diversified product lines in many food and beverage areas. Perhaps you can differentiate between a family business and a family-owned business with the former being smaller and the latter being larger, but a family owns and operates both types regardless of scale and scope of the business. The point here is that work has meaning to an individual and to a group of people. In the case of the family business, that business can dominate the lives of all family members. That is, the meaning of work transcends the individual to the group. In Chapter 1, the issue of work–family conflict was described to demonstrate the power of work in individuals' lives. In a family business, it is easier to see the power of work not just in an individual's live but also in the lives of people working for the same business.

A family business might represent an extreme case to demonstrate the centrality of work to larger social structures, and it is fair to make that point. However, given the number of people working in family businesses, this extreme case might actually represent the norm for most people across the globe. The boundaries between work and non-work or home contexts can be completely obliterated in the context of a family business. Not only does one's work play a central role to how one views oneself, but in a family business, work defines relationships between family members. Individual actions spill over to family actions, and these actions influence the business, which in turn reciprocally impacts the individuals. You can open an Internet search engine and search "family business horror stories," and millions of search results will appear in a second. Some stories focus on issues of family succession for businesses, which might be as tricky as the royal succession in Britain. Some stories focus on failed business relationships spilling over into failed family relationship. Particularly noxious behaviors can be read about in stories focusing on what happens when the divorce of a marriage affects a family business. Not only will families be torn apart but so too will businesses that include multiple family members.

Of course, non–family-owned businesses or corporations will not have this type of exposure. However, even these larger social structures are affected by the work actions of individuals. Consider turnover and retention in organizations. The relationship an employee has with his or her boss is considered by some to be the only relationship that matters inside of an organization. When you have good supervisor – and you will know a good boss from a bad boss when you see them – you are more satisfied with your job and company, you are more committed to your company, and you are less likely to turnover to another employer. The obverse of these relationships is true when you have a bad boss. What happens, though, when your boss gets promoted, retires, or leaves the company for another company? How do you feel about your company? Do you want to stay or leave, too? Whether your boss's decision was planned or unplanned, the reality shock of their leaving will cause you to reassess your future relationship with your company. Your boss's decision will affect your home life. You will talk with your friends and family members about what has happened and how you should proceed. You will spend your quiet hours thinking about the implications of your boss's decision to not just your work but also your life. Being social animals, relationships are important; and work relationships can be just as strong as your non-work relationships. In fact, relationships embed you at your work and in your non-work community. These relationships can predict whether you will stay or leave your employer. Moreover, these relationships explain how turnover and retention decisions can spread from employee to employee.

When your boss or close coworker decides to leave your company, understandably you will begin to think about your long-term prospects with the company. What about when your least favorite coworker or not a particularly close coworker decides to leave? Will their departures affect you in the same way as your boss or close worker leaving the company? While the strength or intensity of your feelings might not be as strong, even the departures of distant coworkers will cause you to think about your long-term prospects within the company. Turnover inside of organizations does not happen in singles, it happens in waves as if spread like a contagious disease. The social relationships act as the accelerant to turnover decisions. The shock of the departure or turnover of an employee acts as the spark. From there, employees begin a rational and predictable process of considering their futures. Luckily for companies, social relationships also act as an accelerant for generating and spreading positive outcomes. Just as turnover can spread through an organization, so too can employee engagement. When an employee becomes immersed and satisfied with his or her work, other employees also become more immersed and satisfied. While it is easier to see the connection between individuals and work or between families and work than it is to see the connection between individuals, work, and large companies, those connections do indeed exist and are quite powerful.

We can continue to broaden out the lens on exploring the centrality of work from individuals to groups, to organizations, and to nations. Nations with developed economies – those most ripe for displacement in the age of automation, artificial intelligence, and machine learning – have laws governing the rights of employees, the relationships between employers and employees, and the relationship between employers and the government. In the previous chapter, we discussed trade unions and guilds, which protect people in specific trades. In some nations, unions and guild – yes, some still exist – possess considerable power in protecting employee rights and how employers can interact with employees. The power of unions, in particular, varies from nation to nation. In the United States, for instance, peak rates of unionization occurred in 1954, with just over 25% of workforce belonging to unions.[2] In 2019, just 10.3% of the US workforce belonged to unions; and more than half of those members worked in public sector jobs.[3] Union rates in Western Europe, on the other hand, can exceed 60%.[4] Unions not only protect employees from unfair management practices but also help to reinforce the role that work plays in an individual's life. Unions can collectively bargain for provisions that allow employees to define the scope of their jobs or how their expertise is expressed on the job. Moreover, unions add yet another layer of social identification to an individual's self-concept. Consider that many union members proudly wear clothing emblazoned with union identifiers. Think about how some unions specifically relate to distinct jobs – plumbers, electricians, masons, and other skilled trades. People who identify with their work will have that identity reinforced by the union. Also, members of these unions spend considerable time with each other outside of the work context and this time together cements these relationships.

National laws related to employment or jobs do not end with unions. Nations, based upon their national cultures, promulgate laws that define under what conditions one can work. Laws can stipulate at what age someone can work. Laws can protect people from being fired or in some cases who can be hired. Nearly every economically developed nation has laws that stipulate when someone can retire from their job, how they will fund their retirement, and how their health needs will be covered while working and after retirement. This is how important work is to societies. Laws will protect citizens in pursuit and achievement of their work.

This is not to say that the formation or application of employment and labor law is an easy process. At the turn of the twenty-first century, much of the Western industrialized world found itself in political turmoil over who could work. In some nations, this took the form of a civil rights movement. Would women find true equality in the workplace in terms of access to work, compensation for work, and a psychologically and physically safe working environment? Would persons of color similarly find equality in the workplace? Would members of the LBGTQ community feel safe, respected, and equal treatment in the workplace? In other nations, strife over immigration had its roots in who exactly would be able to work. Would immigrants – whether they arrived legally or illegally – displace native citizens in jobs? Would they be given perceived preferences for jobs? Would they have access to earned work benefits that governments grant to citizens?

It is important to understand the psychological power of earned work benefits – of which some might call "entitlements" or "social safety nets" – and how these earned work benefits relate to one's work and identification to work. The word "fairness" will inevitably come up when discussing these work-related benefits. Fairness, even if nations attempt to legally define what fairness means in a work context, can be in the eye of the beholder. Since Yale University psychologist J. Stacey Adams formalized what is now known as *equity theory*, academics and practitioners alike have devoted considerable resources into researching the concept of fairness. When an employee believes that his or her hard work has earned specific outcomes – salary, bonus, working conditions, promotion, benefits, and any other outcome you can think of – he or she will also compare the efforts and outcomes of other employees in the workplace. If that employee believes that his or her effort has yielded few outcomes than those in the workplace, that employee might come to believe that the employer has not treated him or her fairly. Objective standards of performance might not matter. Lack of knowledge or insight into others' outcomes might not matter. Comparing one's self to a peer, supervisor, or even executive might not matter. What matters is the employee's perception of fairness. Applied to earned work benefits, one might perceive that others have not worked as hard or "earned" the right to those benefits.

Because work is central to humans, it is central to societies and their governments. While it is easy to focus on negative outcomes in societies related to work, history is replete with examples of the positive power of work to a society. In the aftermath of World War II, most of Western Europe lay in ruin. The destruction to Asian nations was similarly as severe. Even the nations physically untouched by the war had military personnel return from war zones after experiencing the psychological and physical trauma of war. Unlike the aftermath of World War I where the losers of that war struggled to rebuild their societies, national leaders chose a different path at the conclusion of World War II that entailed the role of work in helping both people and societies recover from the war.

The Marshall Plan, named after the United States Secretary of State George Marshall, was an economic recovery plan that the United States initiated to rebuild Western European nations destroyed by the war. The United States released direct monetary aid to help nations rebuild infrastructure and modernize industries. Nations receiving aid agreed to trade compacts, changes in business regulations, and industry productivity goals. That is, the Marshall Plan helped put people to work as a means to rebuild and heal from the war. While not as large as the Marshall Plan, the United States provided economic aid to nations in Asia to help rebuild after the war. Part and parcel with rebuilding nations was the idea that economic recovery would serve to stabilize those nations so that a lasting peace between nations might occur. Work – giving citizens the ability to work, to achieve, to pursue opportunities, to provide resources to live whatever life one wants to live – became a fundamental piece to the recovery of the most devastating war that the world has yet seen.

The stability a nation can achieve is inextricably tied to its economy and the work that citizens do. Going back to Adam Smith, he theorized that the work and commerce done within nations led to the development of political systems to govern those work and commerce processes. Governments could facilitate trade between nations through reducing tariffs or through enacting treaties to ensure the flow of goods, although in Smith's view, such mechanisms involved govern- ments picking winners and losers among industries and nations. This would inhibit a free market where supply and demand are distorted not by the markets but by the govern- ments themselves. Smith's work on the relationship between individuals, work, government, and nations relates now to what we know as economic systems. In a capitalist economic system, employee work and business production are done for private profit – meaning that individuals gain the most from their labors. Governments can regulate business environments and levy taxes on individuals and businesses to fund programs for the greater good of the society, but the government itself does not own the means of production in a capitalist society.

On the other hand, a socialist economic system emphasizes production for use instead of production for profit. That is, the goal of economic activity should be to create value, not profit. Socialist economies require planning and forecasting to more accurately meet supply and demand of products or services, which, under a capitalist society, would be accom- plished by market equilibrium. The key distinction between a socialist economic system and a capitalist economic system comes down to ownership of the means of production: social or individual. It is important to understand that both political economic systems directly relate to individual work and how that work benefits individuals, businesses, and societies.

We should not, however, confuse political economic systems with types of governments. While the United States uses a representative form of democracy for its governing system – that also has a free-market capitalist economic system – Sweden uses a parliamentary form of democracy for its governing system that has a mixed-market economy with a strong welfare state. This means that some industries operate in a free-market capitalist system as other industries operated in a socialist system. For instance, Sweden's automotive industry operates in a free market while its healthcare industry is socialized. In 2014, Sweden's government owned just under 25% of the nation's wealth, whereas the United States' government owned none.[5] China and Vietnam have communist forms of government and mixed economies featuring planned socialist economies that now allow for some free-market activity in some industries. China, for instance, allows private ownership of companies in some cases, while it also owns or is a shareholder of other companies. Both the United States and Sweden have democratic forms of government but have different economic systems to maintain stability in their nations, while China and Vietnam have communist forms of government but have different types of socialist economies to maintain stability in their nations.

In every previous Industrial Revolution, new jobs and industries have displaced those jobs and industries that are outdated. After World War II, the growth of the manufacturing sector of the United States economy led to the development and growth of a stable American middle class and ushered in an era of American prosperity and global power. The growth of China's manufacturing sector has similarly created a stable

Real Worry in This Century

middle class and has sparked the nation's rise as an economic superpower. As the *Fourth Industrial Revolution* accelerates, it is those manufacturing jobs that automation, artificial intelligence, and machine learning will displace. The question is what jobs and industries will be created in the wake of this displacement? The pace of automation, artificial intelligence, and machine learning fundamentally alters the life cycle of jobs and organizations. The job of a telemarketer, for example, has only been around for the last 40 years. In the 2000s, many telemarketing jobs were outsourced to lower labor cost nations. Now that job is being eliminated by robocaller machines with chatbots interacting with live callers. The idea that a job can come into existence and go into extinction in a generation will tax the human ability to adapt and evolve more quickly than was required in the past.

Organizations, too, will have to adapt and evolve as rapidly as automation, artificial intelligence, and machine learning change. As employees have their jobs displaced and will be required to deal with the psychological outcomes of these shocks to their self-concepts, organizations will experience similar stressors. Change is never easy inside of any organization, even those that pride themselves with cultures of continuous change. Ramping up or down production, hiring or laying off employees, creating new product verticals or shuttering old ones, and purchasing new technical systems or mothballing legacy systems takes time. Yet it will be dealing with human effects of change that will likely take the most time to cope with, as the organizational changes trigger secondary waves of employee stress or job turnover. Some jobs will survive the *Fourth Industrial Revolution*, just as some organizations will survive and thrive in it. Others will not!

What happens, however, to societies and nations as the *Fourth Industrial Revolution* accelerates is currently unknown.

In previous industrial revolutions, the changes produced periods of economic instability, unemployment, and social strife that governments responded to in different ways. Social safety net programs expanded and adapted. Ruling governing parties were overthrown and replaced, as national leaders adapted to the new realities that industrial change ushered in. Waves of migration from nation to nation, with people looking for work and better lives, reshaped societies. In some cases, civil wars or wars between nations occurred amid – and some might say due to – the change.

Every industrial revolution creates new industries; until they don't. Before we understand what might happen in this next revolution, it is important to first understand the current state of artificial intelligence, machine learning, and automation and how those will continue to swiftly change over the coming decades.

3

THE CURRENT AND FUTURE STATES OF AUTOMATION, ARTIFICIAL INTELLIGENCE, AND MACHINE LEARNING

To this point in the book, you have seen the phrase "automation, artificial intelligence, and machine learning" and might have assumed that each of those technologies were the same. You might have also assumed that the future of "automation, artificial intelligence, and machine learning" was here and now. Automation, artificial intelligence, and machine learning are in fact different yet related technologies, and at this point in time, those technologies may not be in their infancies but they are not yet fully formed. Let us begin by first differentiating those technologies and follow by examining their current states before getting into their futures.

Automation is the most established technology and business practice of the aforementioned technologies. Automation occurs when a machine, mechanical apparatus, system, or process is run or conducted automatically[1]. That is, there is no human – or in some cases, animal – intervention required to complete the tasks associated with the work being done automatically. Several industries have already seen extensive aspects of jobs automated. Manufacturing, transportation, logistics, defense, utilities, retail, hospitality and tourism, banking, and telecommunications have seen intense automation. Robots long ago displaced human workers on assembly lines in the automotive manufacturing process. General Motors deployed the first industrial robots to perform specific and repetitive tasks in 1961[2]. Robots similarly have replaced some human work activities around loading docks and terminals in the transportation and logistics fields; moreover, some aspects of in-flight pilot work have been automated – through the invention of autopilot technology. Military forces across the globe regularly use drones and other remotely controlled vehicles to reduce the risk of harm to their personnel while carrying out hostile operations. We have become used to automatic teller machines – ATMs – as a means to access currency. When arriving at airports, we seldom think about the work we as customers do in checking in to flights by using digital kiosks that print boarding passes and luggage claim stickers. Why wait in line when you can tag your own luggage and bring it over to the security scanning machine and conveyor belts that send your luggage to the correct gate? Hotels have made it easy and efficient to check into your accommodations, with online check-in sites or on-site kiosks assigning you a room, dispensing keys, and even checking out or billing hotel patrons without ever talking to a hotel employee. Automation has become so ingrained in telecommunications that some people never talk to a representative; instead, a series of push-button menus can guide a customer through any series of complex activities that used to require talking to a representative or even visiting a brick-and-mortar store location. Automation results from humans' innate drive for efficiency, and while we understand that automation has displaced millions of jobs over the years, we see automation as beneficial to lowering costs and providing more efficiently produced goods, services, and systems. Indeed, many of us probably cannot remember a time where automation did not exist or touch our lives, even if only in a tangential way.

Artificial intelligence appeared much later than automation, although perhaps the concept of artificial intelligence has occupied the human psyche or imagination through books or movies. Samuel Butler published the novel *Erewhon* in 1872, where he asked questions about a future of machines having the intelligence of humans. Perhaps even Mary Shelley's *Frankenstein*, published in 1818, first broached the idea of a non–human being containing some level of human intelligence. The 1927 Fritz Lang's German film *Metropolis* included a robot character that acted as a double for a real character. The first machines that were considered to mimic human intelligence appeared during World War II, especially the invention of Alan Turing's codebreaking machines.[3] More than a decade later, however, the phrase "artificial intelligence" was defined and has subsequently been refined to describe machines that respond to stimuli or situations in ways that are consistent with how a human would respond to the same stimuli or situations.[4] This means that machines can exhibit judgment or make decisions that are consistent with human judgment and decision-making.

Artificial intelligence has found footholds in many industries. Banking, healthcare, education, marketing, transportation, accounting and finance, retail, and technical support have all been impacted by the use of artificial intelligence. Banks and financial institutions currently use algorithms to detect fraud and security breach for their customers. They also use "chatbots" – think Siri – that can also respond to texts, emails, and Internet-based messaging to facilitate customer relationships. Healthcare organizations use artificial intelligence to assist in diagnoses, especially in situations where medical professionals lack complete information about a patient. Algorithms identify data patterns that are consistent with certain ailments, which helps doctors to seek more evidence in order to rule in or out possible diagnoses. Artificial intelligence applications greet radiologists with preliminary reports on MRI and X-rays to more accurately and efficiently provide feedback to other doctors and their patients about the extent of injuries. Accountants regularly use algorithms and bots – which can also detect patterns of fraud or data outliers that need further investigation – to assist in auditing processes of large and complex companies. College and university enrollment managers and recruiters can use artificial intelligence applications to crawl through applicant information to find "best fit" applications. In some cases, colleges and universities pair with third-party vendors that have access to large consumer databases who then use algorithms to crawl through millions of individual records to find potential applicants who fit a particular student profile.

When we see or read news stories about Tesla's or Google's refinements of self-driving cars, we might see the connection between artificial intelligence and transportation. We might not see, however, the work of artificial intelligence at play behind managing stoplight patterns on busy roads that help manage the flow of traffic. We might feel the work of artificial intelligence most acutely when we shop online. Amazon uses predictive text to fill in the search box when we type in a product or book we want to purchase. Amazon nicely also recommends other products we might want to purchase based on our last purchase. Facebook and Twitter might integrate with Amazon or Google to then serve us advertisements for products or services that might appeal to us. With so much data available to companies from our past purchases and Internet search histories, marketers can microtarget advertisements down to a single user. Such is the power of the current state of artificial intelligence.

Machine learning takes artificial intelligence to the next level. While artificial intelligence seeks to facilitate machines into making decisions like humans, machine learning occurs when those machines can learn from previous decisions and outcomes to adapt on their own without any human intervention. That is, coders will not have to write additional software code to "teach" the machines what to do in a new situation. The machines will learn to adapt on their own. This is the stuff of movies like *The Terminator*, *The Matrix*, *War Games*, or *Minority Report* that can be simultaneously intriguing and frightening. On the one hand, the machines can radically reduce physical and psychological burdens to humans. On the other hand, what use will humans have if the machines take over so many human activities? The more a machine can learn from itself without any human intervention – usually in the form of coding – the *deeper* the learning becomes. In essence, instead of coders or programmers assisting the machines to learn, deep learning machines will create their own algorithms and link those algorithms into others to form artificial neural networks. The machines can evolve on their own.

As with the applications of artificial intelligence already covered, many industries have started using machine learning – with deep learning and neural network applications – to perform work tasks that humans have traditionally done. In the healthcare industries, doctors and laboratory technicians can feed computers thousands of blood samples to help identify types of bacteria. The machines can then learn on their own to detect new types of bacteria that were not present in the thousands of samples initially provided. A deeper learning application of this example would be for the machines to not only identify the presence of a new bacteria but also to actually diagnose the new bacteria. Chatbots in the banking and finance industries learn from previous customer service interactions to help customers solve new problems. Personal finance apps take user spending and banking information to help users make better daily purchasing decisions. In retail, machines can use real-time customer actions to modify messaging and pricing information that a customer sees. For example, an online shopper might view a product but click off the product to examine something else. An algorithm can send a different advertisement of the same, previously looked at product that contains a different message about the product. The algorithm can also modify the displayed price of the product to persuade the user to move closer toward the purchase of the product. During the COVID-19 pandemic, many consumer product websites did not disable these algorithms, which led to skyrocketing prices on essentials like toilet paper.

When Tesla or Google sends a driverless car on a trip across a country, they are testing the car's ability to learn and adapt to real-time driving. A human might ride along in the passenger seat – computer in hand to assess real-time data and for safety reasons – but the goal is for the car to engage in deep learning so it can learn to drive more safely. Consider also what occurs when you use a smartphone traffic app as an example of machine learning. Your Google Map application does not just map out directions for you to follow but also provides you with real-time updates that affect your destination arrival time. This requires the app to process the movements of other travelers, their rates of speed, and traffic or accidents to adjust your course of action. Amazon Web Services has partnered with the United Kingdom's National Health Service Business Services Authority to deliver combined health, dental, and prescription services. Chatbots and algorithms interact with users to direct them to the proper support services in ways that eliminate wait times.[5] Absorbing millions of pieces of real-time data, assessing courses of action, integrating those actions into systems and networks, and adapting and learning in real time are the current powers of machine learning.

To give you a sense of how much automation, artificial intelligence, and machine learning currently impact industries, it might be instructive to look at the jobs displaced by those technologies and why organizations – not just for-profit but also non-profit – embrace these technologies. Oxford Economics forecasts that 8.5% of the global manufacturing workforce – 20 million workers – will be displaced by automated robots by 2030.[6] A McKinsey study noted that robot prices are three times less expensive than the cost of labor.[7] Brookings Institution estimates that 36 million jobs in the United States have more than 70% of their functions exposed to artificial intelligence replacement using *current* technologies.[8] To give a sense of the business value of artificial intelligence, the retail industry will spend $7.3B *per year* on artificial intelligence by 2022.[9] The healthcare industry will see $150B worth of artificial intelligence activity by 2026.[10] PwC, a global consultancy, estimates that the global economy will see a $15.7T lift from artificial intelligence. The question at hand right now is, "how many jobs will artificial intelligence, machine learning, and automation disturb now and in the future?"

We have a firmer grasp on what jobs these technologies currently affect and which jobs these technologies will not upset. For automation, any job that consists of highly repetitive activities and minimal decision-making or judgment will be a prime candidate for automation. This places factory and manufacturing jobs in prime positions to be automated. The wholesale and retail trade industries will be similarly affected, as will transportation and storage. Unmanned retail stores – using shelf-mounted, sliding robots and check-out kiosks – already exist, fueling a $19B retail automation market by 2023. In the agricultural industries, robots can automate nearly the entire farming cycle of preparing fields, planning seeds, maintaining crops, and harvesting. Food services have already seen extensive automation, from ordering and check-out, through dispensing beverages and even lower skilled food preparation items. Jobs with highly predictable physical work, data collection, and data processing functions are hallmarks of jobs most at risk for automation through robots.

Jobs less susceptible to automation through robots have less routine physical labor, require more interaction, including managing, with employees, customers, or users, and require high levels of expertise. For instance, while assembly line work is ripe for robotic automation, jobs in construction and working with animals are less susceptible to robotic automation. The construction industry is an interesting example of an industry that will be differentially affected by automation. Some jobs within construction that rely more on manual labor – moving materials, digging, pouring concrete, welding, and soldering – will see more automation. However, other skilled trade jobs within the industry – plumbing, masonry, electrical – are less exposed to automation. Those jobs require more expertise and less routine physical work. The work that is least at risk for automation requires high-touch customer or patient work, creative work, work associated with managing or developing other employees, and jobs that require high levels of planning or decision-making. The healthcare industry is illustrative for these types of jobs. On one hand, robots will perform routine tasks such as medical records filing or transporting specimens to and from laboratories. On the other hand, patient-facing jobs – doctors, nurses, assistants – are some of the lowest risk jobs to be automated. Overall, McKinsey and Company, a global consultancy, estimates that in the United States alone, nearly 40% of occupations will shrink between now and 2030.[11] Just as worrying is that those jobs primarily affect employees with less-than-college levels of education.

Artificial intelligence and machine learning will differentially affect jobs and industries. Unlike jobs exposed to automation that tend to be more blue-collar, manual labor types of jobs, artificial intelligence will disproportionally affect high paying, white-collar jobs. To this point, the Brookings Institute estimates that jobs requiring a graduate or professional degree are four times more likely to be exposed to artificial intelligence displacement than jobs requiring a high school diploma.[12] In the preface of this book, we detailed the coming disruption to the accounting industry that is fueled by artificial intelligence – in the form of bots and algorithms. The accounting industry will not be alone. Marketing researchers and specialists will see intelligent software adapt messaging, price, and location information about products in real time. Similarly, algorithms and chatbots will replace some of the work done by financial advisors. Sales managers will see artificial intelligence applications reduce their work tasks, as computer-to-computer interactions will remove what were once person-to-person interactions. Ironically, computer programmers who build automation and artificial intelligence applications will become redundant as the machines engage in deep learning to adapt to real-time situations. In the United States alone, upwards of 70 million jobs are currently exposed to medium and high levels of job displacement due to artificial intelligence applications. Conversely, manual trades like pipe fitters, solderers, and automotive mechanics have limited to no exposure to artificial intelligence displacement. While food servers and cooks might see automation replace parts of their jobs, artificial intelligence applications will not affect those jobs. For human resource management professionals, neither automation nor artificial intelligence applications pose displacement risks. Technologies like robots and artificial intelligence applications will not eliminate all of the jobs in the fields and industries stated above. It is more likely that those technologies will dramatically reduce the size of workforces associated with those jobs. For the human resource management professional, the issue might become more of sifting through a large supply of applicants for fewer jobs. It might be more about developing and retaining highly skilled employees for the human resource management professional.

Machine learning applications, like artificial intelligence applications in general, will ripple through different jobs and industries than automation. It is the deep learning and neural networks that we must focus on in order to understand what jobs and industries will be most upset. As machine learning applications like voice assistants become more refined, these will displace office assistant jobs. Similarly, chatbots will affect call center and front-line customer service jobs as the deep learning and neural networks become more refined. Reading radiology images to detect injuries or abnormalities can be done through machine learning, but the doctor-to-patient discussion cannot. A machine can learn to detect bacteria in blood samples, but an integrated treatment plan for a patient requires human coordination and care. Educators, especially working in online environments, might provide less value in an online threaded discussion that a chatbot might be able to accomplish; but educators will still conduct the primary research that adds to the bodies of knowledge that chatbots can learn to disseminate through those online threaded discussions. Machine learning might not displace workers from jobs – at least not in the near term – as much as machine learning will alter how employees carry out their jobs. That is, machine learning will more likely cause job redesign than job displacement. As with other artificial intelligence applications, machine learning might not eradicate jobs and industries as much as it might reduce the number of employees needed in any of those jobs and industries.

We should not, however, think that the pace of automation, artificial intelligence, and machine learning will displace entire workforces and industries overnight or in a decade. Yes, the global workforce will experience displacement in some jobs and industries, but that will unevenly occur as the technologies underpinning automation, artificial intelligence, and machine learning mature. As we have already described in this chapter, automation, for instance, has heretofore advanced over a period of hundreds of years. The pace of change of automation has increased over the past four decades, and the pace of change for artificial intelligence and machine learning has increased over the past two decades. What can we expect in terms of rate of change for these technologies over the coming decades is an important topic to explore.

The pace of automation – primarily robotics – will be driven by two factors. First, how fast will the technology underpinning advances in robotics advance? Second, what is the business case for adopting those technologies? Just because a robot exists does not mean that a business will adopt its use. Robots currently used in automation largely replace the highly repetitive and manually intensive labor tasks that do not require fine motor skills. That is, you are more likely to find a robot carrying large pieces of materials and affixing those materials to other materials that are in a set or prefabricated position. Think of the robots used in automobile manufacturing. The robotic arms can grab and carry a prefabricated passenger door to an assembly line where the soon-to-finish car is moving down the line. The robotic arm can align the car door to the existing frame of the car while another robotic arm can screw or bolt the door in place. If a human were to do these tasks, it would require large muscle group movements and less fine motor skill movements. This explains why some skilled trades are less exposed to replacement via automation. The smaller the materials used, the more variable the environment, the smaller the spaces between materials, the more difficult it is for a robot to do. Machines certainly help identify problems or diagnose deficiencies, but the robotics – at least at this point in time – have difficulty executing tasks that require finer motor movements, real-time problem-solving, or changing environments.

Consider automobile mechanics. Because modern automobiles contain computers to integrate functions, mechanics utilize computers to run diagnostics to help identify problems. Once identified, mechanics use their physical tools and human skills and effort to fix the problem. They then return to the computer to run more diagnostics to ensure the fix has solved the problem. Consider also a construction site to build a residential home. The construction site needs to be surveyed so that the site can be cleared, so that utilities can be planned and other man-made objects can be inserted, and where other public infrastructure will connect to the new home. Clearing and preparing the construction site requires removing objects, leveling ground, and moving materials to the site. From there, foundations are dug or installed, trenches for utilities are dug, and the actual construction of the home begins. Robots can certainly assist in some of these processes and phases, depending on how integrated the robotics are with other machines. Yet the variability inherent in these processes makes it unlikely that they can be fully automated. This does not even get to the actual construction of the new home. As with automobile manufacturing, robots can replace certain parts of construction. However, as the details of the construction become finer, it becomes more difficult for robots to replace human work.

This does not begin to address the second question to answer about the use of robotics: the business case. The costs of robotics used for automotive manufacturing have fallen dramatically over the past three decades. As costs have fallen and the robots become more adept at assembly line manufacturing, businesses have increasingly used automation instead of human labor. The robots cost less than human labor for these types of work tasks. The robots run more efficiently and for more hours than human labor can. Robots will also make fewer mistakes than humans on these types of tasks. While car prices for consumers may not have dramatically fallen as automation has increased in the automobile manufacturing, the cost of making cars has reduced. The capital investments required to automate more of the assembly line can still be quite steep, but the increased efficiency and reduced human labor costs over time more than pay for these investments. In terms of overall pace of automation, it can take anywhere between 8 and 28 years to complete the cycle of advances in technology and business case for adopting that technology.[12] Right now, it takes about a generation for adoption of automation technology to replace human work. Yet even by the year 2030, automation could displace 29% of jobs in heavily automation-impacted industries while only accounting for 13% of job growth in those industries.[13]

For automation to fully replace human work, machine learning and robotics will have to make continued integrated advances. That is, artificial intelligence and machine learning applications will have to be embedded into the robots that automate human work. The current state of artificial intelligence does not allow for those types of applications. In fact, the current state of artificial intelligence and machine learning are likely decades away from replicating human decision-making let alone being embedded into automated devices. We have already discussed the current state of both artificial intelligence and machine learning, but it is important to understand the pace of development for those technologies and how that pace affects the displacement of workers across industries.

In many ways, artificial intelligence and machine learning have already exceeded human capacity to make decisions and adapt to changing environments – after all a machine has already defeated the best chess players in the world and has bested *Jeopardy* champions Ken Jennings and Brad Rutter. Indeed, Hollywood has already depicted a future of smart cars and traffic grids (*Minority Report*) that allow humans to leave rush hour driving in the hands of machines. Additionally, Hollywood has already depicted a future where smart health machines diagnose and treat humans in real time (*Elysium*). Lastly, Hollywood has already shown a dystopic view of self-aware military machines initiating global thermonuclear war and actively warring with humans over control of the Earth and over both humans' and machines' right to live (*The Matrix* trilogy). Current artificial intelligence applications currently cannot, however, replicate human creativity or caring. Yet machine learning – with deep and neural networks – might in time also allow machines to learn these very human qualities. After all, Hollywood has also depicted a future where self-aware, personalized operating systems become more than just office assistants but become able to form intimate machine–human relationships that are just as complex as intimate relationships between humans (*Her, Bladerunner 2049*).

The more current "narrow" forms of artificial intelligence described in this chapter will at some point give way to what is referred to as "singular" artificial intelligence.[14] Singular artificial intelligence – where machine learning and deep neural networks have freed machines from human programmers and learned to adapt their algorithms in real time – will have the ability to fly unmanned space missions to distant planets and solar systems, conduct full-scale experiments, collect and interpret data and develop new hypotheses, report out important findings, and safely return to Earth. This all will be accomplished without any human intervention. At current rates of investment, research and development, and implementation, the artificial intelligence technologies needed to complete this type of exploration could exist in as soon as 30 years. What happens beyond those 30 years is likely to quicken in terms of the pace of change for artificial intelligence. As machines learn to adapt, first more slowly, previous lessons learned will quicken the pace of future learning. Consider that before 2012, computing capacity for artificial intelligence doubled every two years. Since 2012, that capacity doubles *every three months.*[15] Companies report 10% increases year to year in adopting artificial intelligence into portions of their businesses. The accuracy of machine-learned image recognition has increased more than 20% over the past six years and will exceed 90% accuracy in early 2021. In just two years between 2018 and 2020, the time to "train" machines on imagine recognition has fallen from more than 10 minutes to just under 3 minutes, while the cost of that training over the same time period has fallen from over $2,300 to just $12. In joint reasoning activities, machine learning applications have improved performance just over 20% and is nearing the human baseline accuracy of 80% on these complex reasoning activities. In April of 2019, machines matched human performance on general text understanding and then exceeded the human baseline by nearly 10% just three months later. But are the machines able to fully think like humans?

That answer today is resoundingly no. In fact, right now, artificially intelligent robots possess the general intelligence of that possessed by a rat.[16] If we push far out to the extremes of what we can predict in terms of artificial intelligence, machine learning, and automation replacing or at least being able to replicate what humans can do in almost any job, machines will be able to write a high school essay by 2026, drive a truck by 2027, and work a retail job by 2031. For more creative and complex jobs, such as writing a novel (2049) or performing intricate surgery (2053), the probability of machines out-performing humans in the next 45 years and completely replacing humans at work 120 years from now hovers around 50%.[17] Factors such as public policy and government inter-vention will shape the deployment of automation, artificial intelligence, and machine learning. Much like the questions for business to adopt these technologies, societies will have a say in whether or not the value created by these technologies is worth the cost to humans to remove work from repertoire of everyday human life.

Given the current state of these technologies, their current rate of adoption, and their predicted rate of adoption, we have near-term (within the next decade), medium-term (within the next 50 years), and long-term (100 years and beyond) chal-lenges to consider for their impact on work. The focus of this book – human resources management – will play a vital role across those timeframes as those technologies deepen, and wider applications to the working world are implemented. Over the next couple of chapters, we will offer our best pre-diction of how human resources management will adapt to these stunning technological advances. We begin by detailing how human resources management currently utilizes these novel technologies.

4

THE CURRENT STATE OF HRM WITH AUTOMATION, ARTIFICIAL INTELLIGENCE, AND MACHINE LEARNING

Before peering into the future of human resources in the age of automation, artificial intelligence, and machine learning, a starting point for the current state of the field must first be established. It is not as though human resources management (HRM) has not seen aspects of the field already impacted by the technological trends of the *Fourth Industrial Revolution*. To this point of the book, human resources has rarely been mentioned. How exactly do we define HRM, and what functions do we consider part of this business function? We start by providing a brief overview of HRM and then discuss how the functions of human resources have currently adapted to automation, artificial intelligence, and machine learning.

HRM describes the practices and processes used to attract, develop, retain, and motivate employees within a company or organization. From a strategic perspective, companies deploy their HRM practices and processes in ways to accumulate valuable human capital that is leveraged to help meet companies' missions and goals. That is, HRM practices and processes do not just attract and acquire employees with specific knowledge, skills, and abilities to perform their jobs, but actively work to develop and retain those employees, so that their knowledge, skills, and abilities become a source of value or capital that companies use to create a sustained competitive advantage in whatever industry or market in which any given company competes. Think of human capital as the sum total of all of the knowledge, skills, and abilities of a company's workforce. Theoretically, no two companies will possess the same exact human capital, which means that in practice, human capital is rare and not easily imitated by other companies or competitors. To maintain a competitive advantage derived from human capital, that human capital cannot also be replaced through technological advancements. On the surface, it would seem in the age of automation, artificial intelligence, and machine learning that human capital will be replaced by technology. However, as we established in the previous chapter, not all jobs will be replaced by machines, and the replacement rate of jobs through technology will most likely occur unevenly across industries over the coming decades.

In our current world, human capital can still provide companies with a sustained competitive advantage if companies possess the optimal mix of practices and policies to attract, acquire, develop, retain, and motivate the employees who represent a company's human capital. So how do companies do this through their HRM practices and policies? The traditional functions of HRM include recruiting and selection, which combined are sometimes referred to as a company's staffing practices. The purpose of recruiting – inclusive of the workforce planning – is to attract as many qualified applicants to a job opening as possible. Once an applicant transmits his or her application – whether a resume or formal application –

recruitment ends and selection begins. Selection entails taking all data collected about applicants for a job opening and deciding to hire or not hire those applicants. The data collected during recruiting through a resume, cover letter, or formal application get paired with data collected about applicants during the hiring or selection process. Companies often issue "tests" to applicants, which can include screening a resume, giving personality or other tests, asking applicants to complete a work sample or virtual work session, interviewing applicants, checking applicants' references, or even requiring applicants to submit to background or drug tests, depending on the relatedness to the job. Once the decision-makers in a company determine which candidate they want to hire, they will issue an offer, negotiate terms of employment, and secure a commitment of the applicant to become a functioning member of the company.

Once selection ends with an accepted offer, a company's employee development practices and policies begin. Some companies put newly hired employees through formalized socialization programs where the new hires become acclimated to the company's culture and begin the transition from company outsider to company insider. Such formal socialization programs can be seen as training programs. With training, companies identify specific knowledge, skills, and abilities that current employees lack but require in order to successfully perform the job. The goal of training is to ensure that the identified knowledge, skills, and abilities that are developed through formal training programs will successfully transfer from the training environment to the job and work environment. A company's performance management practices and policies can act to reinforce formal training and then further and continuously develop employee knowledge, skills, and abilities. Performance management is a process of defining and communicating performance expectations, documenting employee performance, and then providing feedback to the employee so that he or she can improve performance. The employee development functions – performance management and training – pair well with employee staffing functions – recruitment and selection – when implementing succession planning programs to identify and develop existing employees for future jobs within a company.

Two additional HRM functions cut across or support the functions mentioned above. Compensation services to attract, motivate, and retain employees consist of two dimensions – direct and indirect compensation. Direct compensation includes monies directly paid to an employee for performing the duties and functions of the job. We typically think of direct compensation in terms of one's salary or hourly wages. Indirect compensation includes all other incentives or benefits that an employee is given for being a member of a company. We typically think of indirect compensation in terms of company-provided healthcare, retirement or pension plans, paid time off, vacation, or sick leave, short- or long-term bonus plans, or a cafeteria buffet of "benefits" related programs like wellness and health programs, childcare support, employee assistance programs, tuition reimbursement, and the like. Whether we talk about direct, indirect, or "total" compensation – the combination of direct and indirect – compensation serves to attract, motivate, and retain employees.

Employment law – and depending on whether or not collective bargaining units operate in a given company – also cuts across or supports the HRM functions listed above. Myriad national laws establish rules and regulations surrounding almost every facet of employment – from reducing discrimination during recruiting, selection, training, performance management, and compensation to how long-term medical or family emergency leave is allocated to protecting pregnant employees from discrimination to how a company enacts layoff of reduction in force actions. Should a company have unions protecting employee collective bargaining units, labor relations become another function included in a company's HRM practices or policies. Finally, some companies, again given the industry or market in which the company operates, will also include occupational health and safety practices and policies under its HRM functions. This function could be linked to training and performance management – whether its ensuring safety in an assembly line setting or proper protocols in a laboratory setting – but can also be a feature of everyday office life where flyers and announcements are posted to educate employees about employee safety protocols, updates for ongoing workplace safety programs, or yearly goals for safety.

All of these HRM functions – recruiting, selection, training, performance management, compensation, employment and labor law, labor relations, and occupational health and safety – can operate independently of each other; however, for a company to truly develop human capital that is rare, unique, and not easily replaced by technology and can be leveraged to meet the company's mission, two crucial things must happen. First, in what is called horizontal strategic HRM integration, each function will mutually support all other functions. That is, what a company does with its compensation practices will necessarily affect its recruiting function. Obviously, job applicants pay a great deal of attention to what a company offers as total compensation during the recruiting process. How a company handles performance management will obviously impact its training programs. Managers are often at the forefront of identifying gaps in employee knowledge, skills, and abilities that can be addressed through training programs. Accomplishing this type of horizontal integration brings to the forefront an often-neglected HRM function – job or work analysis. Job or work analysis is the process of identifying the knowledge, skills, abilities, and functions that are required of the job; moreover, the function also identifies the human qualities or competencies required of the employee in order to complete the job. The ultimate product of a job or work analysis is a position description – sometimes simply referred to as a job description. This product provides an integrative role for HRM practices and policies. After all, if you have not identified what is required of the job, how can you properly develop selection or hiring practices? If you have not identified employee competencies required to complete the job, how do you know what kind of employees to recruit? Without a position description, identifying what knowledge, skills, and abilities are required to properly train employees or assess their performance becomes difficult. Similarly, without a position description, can a company accurately develop and understand the compensable factors that are needed to assess appropriate salaries for jobs?

Horizontally linking a company's human resources functions does not fully realize the value of those practices in creating a sustainable, competitive advantage. Each human resource function also needs to directly link – that is, directly support – the company's mission, which is referred to as vertical human resource integration. Google's company mission states "Our mission is to organize the world's information and make it universally accessible and useful."[1] For Google to achieve vertical human resources integration, each function will be directly linked to that mission. An HR manager overseeing Google's recruitment practices would be able to tell anyone how those practices directly support the mission, as would the HR Managers overseeing the other functions. When a company achieves both horizontal and vertical human resources integration, they will create high performing work systems that attract, acquire, develop, motivate, and retain employees that add value to the company – that rare, not easily imitated, and not easily replaced by technology human capital that the company can leverage like any other capital to achieve its mission.

Understanding exactly what HRM is and how it fits into any company's overall strategy is important as we examine how automation, artificial intelligence, and machine learning impact HRM, even as a system of horizontally and vertically integrated practices. A company *should* consider the systemic effects of these technologies on HRM as they adopt the aforementioned technologies. Whether companies *do* consider those effects is a different story, especially if companies consider the *value* of human resources in the context of overall corporate strategy.

The historical use of automated human resources practices has added considerable value. Consider some of the earliest automated human resources practices. Documentarian Errol Morris's documentary film *The Fog of War* on former US Secretary of Defense, Robert S. McNamara, contains a scene detailing McNamara's use of International Business Machines Corporation's (IBM's) sorting machines to filter punch cards containing attributes of military personnel enlisted in the armed forces during World War II. McNamara's goal in using a machine to automate the sorting of data was to reduce the time required to identify small pools – sometimes of only two or three people – of military personnel to work on highly complex and secret military planning missions. Since the United States' armed forces kept extensive data on each enlisted troop, airman, seaman, or marine that included not just physical attributes like height and weight but also attributes like education level, intelligence, and personality, the Department of Defense had billions of pieces of data from millions of personnel. McNamara sought to find the most talented, conscientious, and intelligent personnel to fill out his planning team, which required him to sort through all of those data and personnel. The IBM sorting machines could do just that in a matter of hours instead of months or years. McNamara's strategic group helped develop sophisticated missions – primarily Army Air Corps missions – that helped hasten the end of the war in the Pacific theater. Automating portions of the selection process reduced the time required to alter military missions.

After World War II, one might have expected the use of IBM sorting machines to dramatically increase in the context of selection or hiring employees. Yet, it was another human resources function that saw more automation. When companies began hiring after World War II, government regulations often required that companies track, compile, and report employment data to government agencies. Often, these data related to compensation issues, particularly payroll and benefits information. Whereas before World War II companies might employ people to collect and file payroll information – to the government for taxation purposes, to banks upon which companies drew funds to pay employees, and to employees in the form of checks with pay stub information on earnings and taxes – after World War II, technological advances allowed companies to automate these processes. Payroll clerks would no longer handwrite or use typewriters to fill in information on checks, record information in files, and in reports to governments. Once employees collected and entered data onto cards or other early forms of computers, the machines could handle the requirements of the payroll and reporting processes.

Similarly, reporting to government agencies for employment and labor law and occupational health and safety compliance became automated after data entry. This type of automation occurred as advances in desktop computing and database storage improved through the 1980s. Standardized forms linked to underlying data to automatically populate fields on these forms. Other technological advancements helped to automate portions of job or work analysis and employee selection. While you might have uneasy flashbacks to your primary, secondary, or college educational experiences when it comes to Scantron response forms, the optical scanning of these "fill-in-the-oval" response forms allowed companies to collect employee- and applicant-provided data and deposit those data into computer database programs. Instead of the old IBM card sorting machine, the optical scanners could collect data and allow human resource professionals to not just sort data but to collate, aggregate, transform, and analyze data. For job or work analysis, job incumbent surveys like the Position Analysis Questionnaire allowed job analysts to collect large amounts of job data, which they could then analyze in different ways and more deeply than they had in the past. For employee selection, the same kinds of data capturing processes allowed recruiters and employee hiring specialists to test applicant competencies like intelligence, as well as attributes like personality. The increased power in database storage, computing, and statistical analyses ushered in an era of evaluating the validity of selection practices. Human resource professionals and academics could more rigorously analyze data from different types of tests to establish validity of those tests. Statistical tools such as meta-analyses helped practitioners establish best practices that could be implemented. Furthermore, the same computing tools helped human resources professionals to better examine the efficacy of employee training programs, as employees could provide assessments of how effective training programs were both during and after training sessions. Companies could also enter yearly employee performance data and subject those data to more rigorous analysis.

Some of this early human resource automation borders on what we might now consider artificial intelligence, but the important distinction to understand is that the technical tools around data collection, storage, computing, and analysis effectively replaced the work that a human might have done in the past. Another aspect of automation to appreciate during this period of time is that automation in other aspects of companies altered how those companies executed their human resources functions. For instance, as robots appeared in assembly lines in the 1980s and replaced human workers, the nature of occupational health and safety changed. Fewer workers operated the machinery of shop floors, which reduced accidents. However, the technicians who repaired robots were now exposed to different occupational hazards and safety concerns.

The next wave of technological advancement occurred through the 1990s as the power of the Internet fundamentally changed how many companies conducted business. Human resources functions fundamentally changed, in response. Perhaps no human resources function changed more during the Dot.Com era than recruiting. Old mainstays of employee recruiting like the newspaper "want ads" section that appeared daily in print quickly converted to online job postings. Companies could also now recruit through their own websites, as job postings and career pages on company websites became universal. Instead of Scantron-type forms and optical scanners, job applicants could fill out applications on a company website or electronically upload cover letters, resumes, and references directly to the company website. All of these data dumped into large databases that managers could then query when searching for best fitting applicants. The Internet in the 1990s became a tool of automation for recruiting. Posting open jobs, providing information about companies, detailing compensation information, and even providing photo tours of facilities did not require a slew of recruiters to reach potential applicants.

Internally within a company, the power of the Internet allowed companies to post compensation and benefits information on secure intranets. Instead of calling the Human Resources Department in a company, an employee could access compensation information – benefits packages, tax information, vacation, or sick leave – from his or her own desk. In the year 2020, this type employee activity is so common that one might forget how these processes happened before this type of HRM automation. What used to take a series of calls or even a visit to a company's Human Resources Department now takes place without interacting with a human resources professional and in a split second.

Another type of automation occurred related to employee training. In the early 1950s, the University of Houston in Texas first televised college courses that students could take toward earning academic credits[2]. The professors would lecture via their classrooms, which essentially functioned as television studios. Students enrolled in this automated delivery of training would submit exams and assignments to professors via mail. This type of knowledge delivery built upon decades, perhaps even centuries of remotely delivering knowledge to users. As early as the 1700s, people could send away for learning materials, often published in books, in order to acquire new knowledge[3]. These developed into what were called "correspondence courses." The trainers in these courses would hold their expertise and deliver that expertise to individual learners via mail. The materials consisted of books or manuals, and the trainers would also mail exams or assignments for the learners to take as a means to assess the transfer of knowledge from the training materials. The individual learners would then send back the materials and any assessment forms to the trainer, who would then certify the successful learners' mastery of the materials. As computing power increased and the advent of personal computing and the

Internet dawned, early online educational programs functioned in this automated, correspondence-type of knowledge
delivery. Companies large and small used these types of
automated training delivery systems and assessments. The US
military[4] still uses traditional correspondence – to supplement
online – courses as part of its employee development
programs.

While employees around the world adapted to these
changes in human resources practices to the point where these
practices became normal, technological advancements in other
facets of peoples' lives began to emerge. Google was founded
in 1997 to help Internet users search an ever-expanding online
world filled with vast and varied amounts of information. In
1994, Amazon launched as a website to connect book readers
with book sellers. LinkedIn appeared in 2003 to help connect
job seekers with companies looking for employees. As depicted in the movie *The Social Network*, Facebook was created in
2004 with goal of connecting college students to each other in
an online forum instead of meeting in person. These companies and the ideas behind them laid the groundwork for a
wave of technological advancements that have pushed automation into artificial intelligence.

What do an internet search engine, an online shopping
website, and two social networks have in common, and why do
these decidedly non-human resources management companies
have to do with human resources? Data. How data are
collected, aggregated, analyzed, and used, however, differs
across HRM functions. Yet, data and the application of data to
make improvements in computing and technology are the
backbone of artificial intelligence and how artificial intelligence
leads to the neural networks that underpin machine learning.

Consider the development of Google and Amazon. Both
companies originated during the computing and technology
boom of the Dot.Com era. Without the Internet – a global

network that connects machines – obviously, these companies could not exist. Before the Internet as we now know it existed, individual computing machines could communicate with each other through dial-up, telephonic technologies. Computer software allowed computers to convert intercomputer signals into data. Clusters of connected computers formed the networks that eventually led to development of the worldwide web as we know it. As information began being stored on the Internet, it became necessary to develop search engines to comb through the sprawling connections of webpages and computers. Google has become the most used search engine in the world with over two trillion searches per day.

Google, however, does more than crawl through webpages to return rank ordering of webpages based upon user queries. Google collects data about user searches. Google collects data about searches related to shopping habits. Google collects data about location searches. Google collects data about scholarly searches. Google collects data about email usage. Google collects data about keyword searches. Google collects data about anything searched, stored, and accessed on the Internet. How Google uses these data are infinite. Advertisers can place ads on webpages or in the results of a user's search. Companies can advertise in user's Gmail accounts. Companies can purchase data from Google for their infinite usage.

Amazon, while not a search engine like Google, serves a different function for Internet search. While you can still search Amazon for books, Amazon has become the world's largest shopping store. It connects buyers and sellers across the world for almost any product one could imagine. In order to use Amazon, a user must provide personal data – name, mailing address, email address, credit card information – to complete purchases. Therefore, not only does Amazon possess data about your purchases and for what you search but also possesses more valuable data than even Google collects.

Amazon can estimate personal finance based upon a user's location and purchasing habits. These factors also allow Amazon to predict a user's educational background and race or ethnicity. These types of data can be purchased, clean of user names or personal identifiers, by other companies who are interested in myriad business ideas or products.

LinkedIn and Facebook capture, collect, and sell even more targeted data. LinkedIn originated as a website to connect job seekers and employers. Job seekers input their locations, educational backgrounds, work histories, and job experiences. Companies input information about their locations, jobs, organizational cultures, and their current employees. LinkedIn has morphed from job opportunity clearinghouse into a network of people and companies. Once users started connecting with each other to clearly identify their "links" to each other, LinkedIn's data took on an even richer component. LinkedIn's marketplace for data includes user data and relationship data. The social network aspect of LinkedIn followed the development of Facebook as the first large-scale social network. Facebook has over *two billion* users – interestingly, if Facebook were a country, they would be one of the largest countries in population on earth – with their Instagram product also having *one billion* users, and their messaging application WhatsApp having nearly *two billion* users. Across these platforms, Facebook not only captures personal information – names, locations, work history, educational history, interests – but also captures social connections, messaging information, and real-time location information. Facebook can also capture user's product purchasing preferences – either through its "marketplace" or about what users post. Every "like" a user issues about a product, page, or comment can help Facebook form a profile of each user. Companies, especially in their marketing departments, value these types of rich data in order to microtarget potential customers for their products.

While specifically highlighting these companies as exemplars of modern companies that collect data, we do not mean to suggest that these companies are the only companies collecting data that is now used not just in marketing companies or products but also in advancing HRM as a field. Credit card companies and rating agencies have long secured users' data and sold those data to companies. What has changed now, however, is the ease of collecting personal data and how these data are aggregated, analyzed, and displayed to help people make decisions. The human resource function within organizations have benefitted from the ubiquity of data just as other business functions have. The pairing of hardware for data storage, software for data collection and analysis, and the connectivity of the Internet has transformed how business is done and that includes HRM. These advancements have set the stage for artificial intelligence applications across human resources.

At the front end of HRM, functions like job analysis, workforce planning, recruiting, and selection have seen varying levels of artificial intelligence adoption. From a strict job analysis perspective, that function of collecting data about the job and the job incumbent produce two products that combine to form a position description. The *job description* details the functions and duties required of the job, while the *job specification* details the knowledge, skills, abilities, and competencies that the job incumbent must possess in order to perform the functions and duties defined in the description. To date, applications of artificial intelligence are not seen in developing the job description. However, artificial intelligence applications do exist in detailing the job specification[5]. Employers collect data around employee competencies and backgrounds during recruiting, which can then be data-mined with algorithms to determine the exact specifications required by the job. What begins as a retrospective analysis of data collected in other human resources functions becomes forward looking or predictive as artificial intelligence applications mine data.

Similarly, much of the data collected around workforce planning begins through retrospective analysis of data. Companies have long used historical data about employee hiring and turnover and paired those data with myriad business data – seasonal sales trends, peak and off-peak employee head counts, labor availability, revenue, and the like – to understand appropriate staffing levels. Developing algorithms to provide staffing scenarios is a tailor-made application of artificial intelligence to this part of human resources, which funnels into how companies then recruit and select the employees for positions that the planning specifies.

Perhaps no other human resources function currently utilizes artificial intelligence applications more than recruiting. The technological advances discussed earlier in this chapter – data collection, organization, and analysis – paired with the availability of job applicant information from company job pages, Google, Amazon, LinkedIn, Facebook, and the like funnel into company enterprise resource planning platforms or large databases that can be mined using algorithms to identify the best fitting applicants for any job opening. Companies still use traditional recruiting methods like job fairs, college recruiting, newspaper ads or billboards, and referrals; but the availability of data from multiple sources allow companies to proactively seek applicants who they then recruit to apply for jobs. Consider an example from higher education. Admission recruiters for graduate programs can attend graduate school fairs hosted by other academic institutions or professional organizations. They can purchase applicant information from Graduate Management Admission Test (GMAT) or Graduate Record Examinations (GRE) and email or snail mail information to possible applicants.

They can set up information sessions at their universities and publicize those sessions via television, radio, newspapers, or billboards. They can even use Google Ads, Twitter, Facebook, and Instagram to promote those sessions. However, those same admission recruiters can partner with third-party streaming music and video vendors like Pandora or Spotify to hypertarget applicants that fit known demographic factors of someone who is likely to be looking to attend graduate school. Those services, which collect user data, can target down to the zip code level when tracking where their listeners are located and can deliver audio and video ads to users that fit preselected demographics. Those same admission recruiters can also partner with data firms that purchase large datasets from vendors. Those firms can take five years' worth of previous applicant information from universities to create profiles of "typical" students for a single university program. The data firms then create an algorithm to crawl through their large databases to identify the "typical" student from those databases. Those "typical" students will then receive an email to learn more about a specific university. The "typical" students can click on a hyperlink in that email which will take them to a unique web landing page that has customized information about the specific graduate program at a specific university. This type of process operates in the background of the admission recruiters' other processes and practices. They need not tend to the algorithm or landing pages until an applicant provides more information, upon which the admission recruiters will then make personal contact.

This type of activity plays out on a large scale every day across the globe. Recruiters provide keywords that search into large databases of job seekers, and the algorithm returns current job seeker profiles that fit the job for which the recruiters are looking to fill. Algorithms can search existing databases of pervious applicants for prior job vacancies to identify possible well-fitting applicants for completely different jobs. Teams of digital experts track possible applicants from information gleaned from applicants' own Internet search histories and their perusing of company websites, which contain embedded digital "cookies" – bits of programming code – that allow the perused websites to track back visitors to their websites. These digital experts then utilize algorithms to sift through all of these collected data to identify possible best fitting applicants that are then contacted, usually via email, to encourage those possible applicants to apply. Social media sites like Facebook and LinkedIn allow digital recruiters to hypertarget possible applicants based upon the very information that users of those sites self-disclose. This type of data mining for passive applicants – people who might not even be looking for new employment but use those social media platforms for personal and professional reasons – complements what more formal recruiters do. That is, while artificial intelligence applications run in the background to identify passive applicants, traditional recruiters will still post job openings on these websites to encourage active job seekers to apply for vacant positions. LinkedIn even provides features for job seekers to signal to possible employers how active their search efforts are and gives employers direct communication channels for applicants to contact them. Of course, LinkedIn retains the good old-fashioned ability to social network and generates referrals from contacts in their networks. Applicants and employers can also utilize these types of features and functions in Facebook and other job search websites.

Yet even with the more active recruiting, the underpinning of web-based recruiting is still data. Moreover, web-based recruiting in and of itself creates a system where more data are collected about applicants – how long did they linger on a webpage, how many pages did they read, how many times did they visit a webpage or job posting, how many employee profiles did they visit? These additional data give companies the ability to fine-tune information they present on webpages or job postings – are messages clear, does information need to appear sooner in a job posting or webpage, are applicants viewing competitor pages or postings, are company compensation and benefits attractive? In a sense, more data beget more data, as the algorithms and data scientists behind them learn to adapt and adjust to increase applicant yields.

The current capabilities of artificial intelligence applied to employee recruiting do not remove humans in the process. Automated systems and artificially intelligent software remove highly repetitive and lower skilled facets of jobs that recruiters used to complete – responding to emails, confirming receipt of applicants' information, disseminating applicant information internally within the company – which makes the process timelier and more efficient. Even the more complex algorithm-based solutions in the recruiting context still require human contact. Recruiters still query databases using keywords, they still read through applicant materials that were identified via keyword searches, and they still make decisions about which applicants will move forward to the next phase of the staffing process. Of course, efficiency in recruitment processes means that fewer humans will be hired to execute the recruitment function, and the introduction of artificial intelligence applications means that human resources departments need to hire data scientists to design the software solutions that recruiters will use, which transforms the composition of HRM departments.

After an applicant formally applies for a job, recruiting and selection begins. Selection fundamentally is a decision-making process, which at this point of time is still made by humans. However, artificial intelligence applications help in the decision-making process. Artificial intelligence applications have already reduced some of the human touchpoints in this decision-making process. For instance, those same keywords that recruiters can utilize in LinkedIn to search for possible applicants can also be used by hiring managers to filter the number of applicants whose resumes will be seen[6]. The algorithms behind the keyword searches will effectively screen out applicants who do not have the knowledge, skills, abilities, experiences, or credentials to meet the requirements of the job. This reduces the time that resume screeners will spend reviewing applicant materials, which, for many applicants, means that their resumes will never be seen by human eyes and they will be excluded from the hiring process.

Artificial intelligence applications are also being used to screen employees during interviews, whereby software uses applicants' computer, phone, or tablet cameras to assess, in real time, applicant facial expressions, body language, voice quality to help managers assess applicant employability[7]. Chatbots and artificial intelligence applications regularly communicate with applicants via text or email to help schedule interview times and locations, as well as answer basic questions about the job. Companies can now also use integrated personality and intelligence tests that applicants receive and must complete as they go through the hiring process. These tests help match company preferences for employee traits with applicant traits, and applicants can be filtered out of the hiring process before a hiring manager sets eyes upon any applicant resumes. Instead of asking applicants to visit the company to complete a work sample test – that is, complete actual job functions in real time to be assessed by a hiring manager – companies can use virtual artificial intelligence programs to accomplish those tasks remotely and online[8]. Along the lines of work sampling and integrated personality and intelligence testing, artificially intelligent "gamification" applications present applicants with what appear to be brief online games that actually analyze, assess, and report on applicants' memory, recall, and ability to apply the information just learned[9].

Once applicants receive and accept offers of employment and join companies, artificially intelligent HRM systems do not end. An array of artificial intelligence applications now enables companies to help develop employee performance through performance management systems. Companies that gather and store data around employee performance can mine those data to look for patterns in employee performance, whether those patterns are indicative of good or poor performance. These data mining algorithms can also account to job and unique job context effects – location, level within a company, managers, product lines, customers, and the like. Identifying employee performance patterns can allow companies to intervene sooner to correct, redirect, or reinforce employee work behaviors[10]. The ubiquity of mobile phones and tablets in the workplace also provide companies with opportunities to track employee movement and location to understand – almost from an ergonomic perspective – if employees can have their work practices better optimized for efficiency. Software applications complement this type of process efficiency-seeking, as software can integrate with employee mobile or desktop work tools to gather data about employees who utilize those work tools. Most importantly for performance management, artificial intelligence applications can provide immediate performance feedback to employees – through text or email messages or even through chatbots[11]. Artificial intelligence software can already facilitate and enhance employee goal setting plans, even ones that include multisource, 360-degree feedback data[12]. This then provides links to how artificial intelligence applications in performance management can also feed into succession planning and workforce staffing algorithms to track an employee's entire career progression. These types of artificially intelligent performance management applications also complement company compensation systems, such as identifying patterns of performance or other employee behaviors that resulted in increased job performance and employee retention[13]. In this case, managers can identify employee performance that trigger merit bonuses or employee behaviors that indicate possible turnover that retention bonuses can mitigate.

The power of artificial intelligence in employee training has been evident for years. The movement of training into virtual reality has already shaped some industries, such as airlines, where pilots spend hundreds of hours in high fidelity cockpit simulators to practice myriad positive and negative situations. While artificially intelligent chatbots have already started to displace the need to train frontline on customer service skills, simulators and role-playing software help to train employees in high-touch customer service settings. Importantly, artificially intelligent software can identify learning styles and optimize the delivery of content based on those learning styles[14]. The same software can provide instant performance feedback during training sessions – even in the form of a virtual tutor.

Finally, human resources professionals responsible for overseeing employee safety also currently benefit from artificial intelligence applications. While automation and artificial intelligence have already removed highly repetitive – causing wear and tear injuries – and potentially dangerous jobs and tasks from employees, specific artificially intelligent applications exist to help identify, track, and report employee safety issues. Algorithms can search text and email for patterns related to harassment. Wearable technology with artificial intelligence software can track employee biometrics to identify strain or unhealthy working conditions[15]. Interconnected devices on shop floors – think Internet of Things – can identify hazards in the workplace before humans come into contact with those hazards[16]. The workplace becomes safer because artificial intelligence helps to predict safety issues before employees are harmed.

While this chapter has not provided a comprehensive list or detailing of all artificial intelligence applications currently utilized in HRM, the field itself has already adopted the use of artificial intelligence to increase efficiencies, reduce errors, reduce accidents, and reduce company costs. Like most business functions, the human resources context is ripe for both artificial intelligence advances but also ripe for employees being displaced by machines. While this chapter presents the current state of automation and artificial intelligence in human resources, the next chapters begin to explore the future of these technologies over the next decades.

5

NEAR-TERM HUMAN RESOURCES CHALLENGES IN THE AGE OF AUTOMATION, ARTIFICIAL INTELLIGENCE, AND MACHINE LEARNING

At the end of the 1986 movie *Ferris Bueller's Day Off*, the titular character tells the audience "life moves pretty fast. If you don't stop and look around once in a while, you could miss it." The whirl of your work and home life can leave you unaware of the technological advances happening every day that will disrupt your life. Earlier chapters in this book described the pace of technological changes associated with automation, artificial intelligence, and machine learning while also describing how the human resources function within organizations has adapted to those technological advances. The scope of this chapter focuses on the near-term – defined as the next 10–20 years or roughly a generation – advances of automation, artificial intelligence, and machine learning and how the human resources function must adapt to the corresponding changes that these technological advances will have on people. The changes will come quickly, and this is your chance to observe, think, and plan for how these changes will impact your organization before you miss it.

To recap some of the pace of change of technology from previous chapters, the effectiveness of robots improves as quickly as every eight years but can occur more slowly out to almost 30 years. The decision to use robots to automate work will always come down to the key factors already discussed: the improvement of technology and the business case to use robots. These two interdependent and reciprocal factors will spur investment into research and development for next-generation robots. As demand for those next-generation robots increases and efficiencies in producing those robots improve, the cost of those next-generation robots will decrease. This will make the business case for adopting robots to automate jobs easier. This is an important point to reiterate: the cost of purchasing robots and reengineering workspaces and processes must be significantly lower than the cost of employing humans to do jobs in order for any company to choose to automate work processes. That is, the juice has to be worth the squeeze.

For artificial intelligence and machine learning, the pace of improvement for those technologies is more rapidly increasing. Again, consider that right now artificially intelligent machines possess the intelligence of a rat. Over the next 20 years, artificially intelligent machines and applications will be able to write a high school term paper, drive a truck, and work retail in a store. Narrow artificial intelligence (highly specialized machines and applications) will not become singular (the interconnected, deep learning, neural networks that are hallmarks of machine learning) for another 30 years. To give you a different sense of how quickly this integration of machines that require human coding in narrow artificial intelligence way, the Internet of Things doubles every four years.[1] Recall that the Internet of Things is the networking of single devices, machines, or applications into an integrated network that can coordinate the activities of those devices, machines, or applications. This is what creates the singular artificially intelligence network of computers and machines that can acquire, analyze, and interpret new data in real time to then adjust without needing human coders to "teach" the machines to respond in ways that humans would expect. Moving from the intelligence of a rat to the intelligence of a human will take decades, but the learning capabilities of the machines will increase leaps and bounds.

What this means for the global workforce in the near term – over these next 10 to 20 years – is millions of jobs will be displaced. As detailed earlier in this book, automation will replace nearly nine percent of the global manufacturing workforce – or roughly 20 million jobs. Automation will produce 13 percent job growth but will cause 29 percent job contraction across industries. Artificial intelligence will displace anywhere between 36 and 70 million jobs in the United States alone, which could result in the contraction of 40 percent of current occupations. Life, indeed, will move fast, out of necessity.[2]

This rapid transition of jobs and occupation and its impact on the global economy will ripple through societies in ways that we have seen in past revolutions and have recently experienced in the COVID-19 pandemic. With automation, artificial intelligence, and machine learning first displacing highly routine – both physical and cognitive – jobs, lower-earning citizens of societies will first experience job displacement. Laborers, assembly line workers, truckers and taxi drivers, retail workers, warehouse employees, and call center employees will find that competition from robots is too difficult to overcome. Chatbots will replace call center employees or customer service representatives. Robots and self-checkout kiosks will replace retail workers. Self-driving trucks with integrated off- and on-loading robots will replace truck drivers and warehouse employees. Self-driving cars will replace taxi drivers and be detrimental to the business models of Uber, Lyft, and other rideshare companies. In service- and consumer-based economies, the contraction or displacement of these types of jobs will significantly impact the working poor and lower-middle class disproportionally.

What does that do to a society? Consider the last two significant global recessions, which occurred in 2008 and 2020. The 2008 "Great Recession" occurred in the aftermath of the collapse of the global financial system after the housing market in the United States collapsed. The National Bureau of Economic Research pegged the start of the recession in December 2007, but the abrupt shuttering of the venerable financial institution Lehman Brothers in September 2008 triggered widespread panic across global financial markets. In the United States during that September, more than 430,000 employees lost their jobs; and the velocity of job losses accelerated to over 803,000 by January 2009. The United States did not see a net increase in jobs until November 2009. Job losses in Canada lagged the United States, as the financial market collapse rolled through that nation. Canada saw its first net job losses in November 2008 and saw its highest monthly job loss peak of 129,000 jobs in January 2009. Canada did not see net job gains again until January 2010. In the United Kingdom, job losses hit 208,000 citizens by the end of 2008 and would peak at over 800,000 combined lost jobs from the start of the recession until April 2010. The Eurozone saw extensive job losses during the Great Recession. Ireland's unemployment rate rose from 4.2 percent in 2007 to 14.3 percent by March 2011. That meant more than 300,000 job losses over a four-year period. Spain's 9.6 unemployment rate at the start of 2008 ballooned to nearly 27 percent by the start of 2013. Similar patterns of job loss occurred nearly everywhere across the developed world, with the notable exception of Germany, which saw only a brief 0.5 percent increase in unemployment during the Great Recession.

The COVID-19 recession harkens back to a more severe and longer lasting global recession, the Great Depression, which began in 1929 and lasted almost a decade in many parts of the world. The COVID-19 recession began in response to a novel coronavirus outbreak in China that spread into a global pandemic. Many nations responded to the public health crisis by enacting strict stay-at-home public decrees to stop the spread of the virus. These stay-at-home orders resulted in the shuttering of vast portions of nations' economies. From January 2020 through May 2020, global markets shed trillions of dollars of economic activity. In the United States, more than 30 million jobs were lost in just two months. In Canada and Australia, more than a million jobs were lost in each nation over that same time period. New Zealand saw its unemployment rate jump from 4.5 percent to over 10 percent. Britain saw 23 percent of its total workforce furloughed by the end of April 2020. The total effects of the COVID-19 recession are unknown at this point in time, but economists predict a many years' long recovery.

Now consider that automation, artificial intelligence, and machine learning were already predicted to displace more total jobs over the next two decades than either of the recessions mentioned above. In fact, the use of machines to conduct work might increase in velocity as a result of the COVID-19 recession. The two aforementioned recent economic recessions and their impact of labor markets, however, is instructive to understand how the technologies of automation, artificial intelligence, and machine learning will shape societies, individuals, and organizations. Instead of a period of rapid job loss and gradual job gains that we see during relatively brief time periods of economic recessions, the adoption of these technologies will create a constant roiling of labor markets for decades. Some research suggests that these technologies will destroy more jobs than they create, while other research suggests that, like every other industrial revolution, the Fourth Industrial Revolution of automation, artificial intelligence, and machine learning will create more jobs than it will wipe out.[3, 4]

Imagine in the not-too-distant future where millions of jobs are abolished and millions are created each year over a decade or two due to technological advances. Typically, this type of job churn happens over the course of a 10-year period, not over a year-to-year comparison. In some ways, this type of churn will feel like what occurs during recessions where millions of jobs disappear but then slowly those same jobs reappear as supply–demand issues find equilibrium. That is, for instance, in the 2008 recession that saw millions of real estate and real estate finance jobs evaporate almost overnight, many of those jobs rebounded once the finance and housing markets stabilized and grew postrecession during the recovery periods. With the *Fourth Industrial Revolution* some jobs will permanently disappear, phased out over comparatively short periods of time as technological advances create new jobs.

As seen in these recent global recessions, job loss affects more than just the individual employee or employee's family. In Spain during the 2008 recession, youth unemployment skyrocketed to levels that scarcely anyone could recall occurring. When 50 percent of any demographic group becomes unemployed, the larger society will experience repercussions across multiple fronts. Poverty increases among the affected group, which triggers a host of challenges that include food insecurity, housing shortfalls, addiction, self-harm, more crime, and increased violence. In the United States after the 2008 recession, many young people who had previously lived on their own were forced to move back into their parents' houses, which created financial and social strains on those family units. The high levels of job displacement also created the environment where government protests sprung up across multiple countries. When citizens experience systemic challenges, they turn to their governments for solutions. In some cases, solutions were neither apparent nor obvious.

During economic recessions, aggregate economic demand falls. If individuals lose employment and the income associated with that employment, a large portion of demand for goods and services decreases. In the 2008 recession, not only did individual demand decrease, but demand from business-to-business interactions decreased as well. That recession originated in financial sectors of economies. Financial institutions saw their balance sheets turn negative and made it impossible to extend credit to other businesses. The drying up of the credit markets ground businesses to a halt. Payrolls could not be met. Cash reserves were depleted. Loans or bonds could not be secured to bridge financial obligations from one month to another. As companies shuttered from the lack of individual and business demand, more and more companies filed for bankruptcy and ceased operations. With individual and business demand severely impacted, that left many governments as the last sources of demand to keep economies running.

Unfortunately, not every nation affected by the 2008 recession entered the recession in healthy financial standing. As Michael Lewis detailed in his books, *The Big Short: Inside the Doomsday Machine* and *Boomerang: Travels in the New Third World*, some national governments did not possess the resources that would allow them to deliver enough fiscal stimulus to individuals and businesses so as to bolster aggregate demand. They simply could not borrow money from other nations or financial institutions because they entered the recession already in poor fiscal positioning and few nations or institutions would chance lending money to them. Some nations responded to the fiscal crisis through massive debt-fueled borrowing from less distressed nations and set about repaying those debts even if it meant post-recession fiscal austerity. That fiscal austerity facilitated a much slower recovery. Some nations met the recession through a mix of public works projects and fiscal stimulus to stimulate both employment and individual and business demand. Banks and other financial institutions received direct government funding to unfreeze credit markets. Some nations, however, saw their central banking systems completely implode and their economies completely ground to a halt. No government spending. No borrowing. Just the need for a complete restart of the economy.

Every country affected by the 2008 recession responded differently to the recession, and each country experienced different outcomes. Spain, for example, saw months of violent protests, fueled by younger citizens who found themselves unemployed and with little hope of employment for years. Iceland transitioned away from a larger financial sector in its economy to recast itself as a global tourist destination. The United States muddled through years of slow economic growth and a recovered job market, while also seeing the rise of nationalism in one of its major political parties. Ireland – once the roaring Celtic Tiger – faced years of government austerity and slow economic growth as it balanced its national budget. Germany, which did not allow the domestic real estate and financial instruments that seeded the global recession, came out of the recession quickly and strengthened its global and political positioning as a world leader.

The effects of the 2008 recession could still be seen as the COVID-19 recession hit in 2020. Youth unemployment meant that a generation of people across the world lost years of wealth accumulation. Instead of fully participating in the economy, millions of young people opted out of traditional markers of financial stability. Real estate purchases among young people plummeted and never rebounded. Ridesharing became the norm as many people decided that car ownership or leasing made little financial sense. Income inequality increased between generations. Trust in governments receded, as social safety net programs like unemployment insurance were not robust enough nor did they last long enough to help citizens return to prerecession lifestyles. Individuals who lost months or years of employment saw their work-related skills dissipate, which led to longer periods of unemployment. Gaps in an individual's resume became more difficult to explain. In parts of the world, drug addiction increased and became an epidemic of its own.

Because companies operate in the confines of nations, companies, too, saw permanent changes in how they operated – especially human resources functions – in response to the 2008 recession. After that recession, the *Gig Economy* came into existence. The concept of temporary employment or contract employment did not begin after 2008. Companies have used those types of staffing strategies for decades. Whether it be the secretary pools in the 1950s or hiring contract employees in the 1980s, companies have always sought ways to meet staffing demands that allowed them flexibility and cost savings. The 2008 recession, however, brought a new mentality to job seekers. Instead of seeking traditional full-time employment, many job seekers sought to patch together part-time jobs – like music bands seeking gigs – to meet employment needs. The *Gig Economy*, then, became a matching of company flexibility and cost needs with job seekers' employment needs. As companies sought part-time or fractional hours of work, job seekers sought to patch together enough gigs to essentially create full-time work. In some nations that provide universal health care, for instance, gigging for employment functions differently than in nations that do not provide universal health care. Gigging for employment in nations with weaker social safety net programs contains significantly more individual risk for job seekers.

From a human resources perspective, the ebb and flow of labor demand in response to economic recessions can often be predictable. As recessions come and companies shed employees and jobs, human resources professionals in financially distressed companies will focus on internal human resources functions. As part of larger company cost-saving strategies, human resources professionals will engage in workforce planning strategies like furloughing, laying off employees, or permanently separating employees from the company. Some of these staffing strategies require data gathering around employee performance. Some companies might choose to furlough, lay off, or terminate employees based upon employee performance or amount of work completed. Some companies might choose to furlough, lay off, or terminate employees based upon seniority, whether or not a union contract exists that specifies seniority as a criterion to make those decisions. Human resource professionals might also explore training opportunities during these workforce planning strategies because remaining employees might require training to perform new functions that were previously completed by other employees. Human resource professionals will examine employee compensation levels or benefit programs to look for cost savings as distressed companies seek to reduce costs and continue operations. During the 2008 recession and COVID-19 recession, you could expect this type of human resources activity to occur in response to the financial and employment crisis.

Even during economic recessions, however, some companies remain in a position to continue hiring. For that matter, even companies experiencing distress will look to selectively hire based on specific needs. During economic downturns, the number of people looking for employment obviously increases. Companies that hire will experience a massive wave of applicants. Again, using the 2008 recession as an example, at the start of the recession in the United States, there were 3.5 unemployed workers per job opening in the nation.[5] According to Glassdoor, companies already receive 250 applications per job during low unemployment conditions.[6] During high unemployment conditions, that number will expand as more unemployed individuals must test the job market. On one hand, this presents companies with opportunities to choose highly skilled employees from the expanded applicant pool. On the other hand, how does a company handle the wave of applicants when applicant pools expand?

Bring this back to the issue of the expected churn of jobs when automation, artificial intelligence, and machine learning continue to mature and accelerate over the next 20 years, human resource professionals might expect two scenarios. One is consistent with how human resources functions during recessions. The other is consistent with how human resources functions during periods of economic growth and stability. That is, during the *Fourth Industrial Revolution*, human resource management departments must operate with flexibility to handle both prosperity and austerity at the same time. Why is that?

Going back to the question of how human resources handles waves of applicants for open positions during recessions, as of 2020, they use artificial intelligence applications to sift through applicants. On the applicant end of the system, websites and hiring apps make it easy to apply for open positions. Job applicants can store their resumes and profiles on cloud-based platforms, and when a position opens, the applicants simply hit "send" for their materials to transmit to the hiring company. Applicants don't need to necessarily think too much about how well they fit the job or the company seeking to hire. They simply see an opening and apply. The hiring company will sort through the applications and make decisions about which applicants will progress through the selection process. That is, technology makes it easy for applicants to no longer consider issue like fit. That is up to the companies to determine at the early stage of hiring.

The same application technologies also make it easier for companies to seek passive candidates who might fit the job or company. LinkedIn provides a "signal" that applicants can activate to let possible hiring companies know that they are interested in exploring different job opportunities. Companies can also use LinkedIn to sift through possible applicants who do not activate that job seeking "signal." Algorithms allow companies to seek out passive job seekers while also sorting through hundreds of applications that are transmitted by active seekers. As machine learning becomes more refined and programmers are no longer needed to provide the coding upon which artificial intelligence operates, the algorithms will automatically adjust to seek applicants and sort through applications. With millions of jobs – upwards of 70 million from automation and artificial intelligence – expected to be displaced over 20 years, companies will remove 3.5 million jobs each year between 2020 and 2040 due to those technologies. If positive projections prove realistic, at least that many jobs will be created by the same technologies that are destroying jobs. Meaning, in addition to any regular hiring during normal business cycles and despite any economic recessions, human resources professionals each year over the next two decades will simultaneously handle millions of employee outplacing activities while handling millions of new hires for jobs that do not exist in 2020.

Thus, we will see a paradox happening within human resources management. The technological forces driving the displacement of jobs will reinforce the use of those same technologies among human resources management professionals across the globe. Workforce planning will become more difficult and require technological assistance through artificial intelligence and machine learning. Algorithms will crawl through job descriptions, position announcements, and employee productivity data to identify jobs that contain features that will be automated or replaced through computers. These same algorithms will also crawl the Internet – including social media platforms – to identify patterns in other companies' job postings to understand how jobs are changing while also capturing how people talk about their jobs changing. Algorithms will seek out new products or technologies that could be acquired so that human employees will become redundant. The same algorithms will constantly monitor the development, capabilities, and pricing of robots that could automate jobs. Much like setting up a Google alert, algorithms will seek out data that help indicate job and technology change and report those alerts to company decision-makers. This will form the leading edge of how a company will understand the displacement of jobs from technologies associated with the *Fourth Industrial Revolution.*

Meanwhile, inside of companies, devices will continue to connect and share data – the Internet of Things will continue to strengthen. Employee productivity information will flow from their workstation computers, tablets, smartphones, and wearable technology. Algorithms will crawl through videos of manufacturing shop floors and retail floors. Algorithms will assess the quality of communication between employees and between employees and customers. What employees do, what they read, who they talk to, how they talk to people, how much time they spend on tasks will all provide a steady flow of data about employee performance. All of these data will form baselines for employee performance. Managers or chatbots will provide constant performance improvement feedback to employees, which, theoretically, should improve employee performance for the better.

The same algorithms that crawl through external websites and data sources looking for changes in jobs and technologies will also gather data about compensation and benefits. These external data will pair with internal data to help balance internal and external equity concerns that permeate current compensation systems. Even as companies outplace employees over the next two decades as jobs become automated or replaced by computers, they will still be hiring employees. Thus, they need to ensure that their compensation systems match what competitors do with compensation and benefits while also ensuring that within the company, pay systems are fair. *The Fourth Industrial Revolution* could be used to help address and improve fairness issues that often arise in the administration of companies' compensation systems. This include reducing pay inequality between genders and ethnicities that plague companies.

The use of chatbots will not just help in performance management but also assist in employee training. As jobs change over the next 20 years, some jobs will require additional technical skills that will improve employee performance. Instead of eliminating jobs, automation, artificial intelligence, and machine learning will require augmenting knowledge, skills, and abilities of current jobs. As seen in the COVID-19 pandemic when virtual meetings on video became a primary mode of communication, many forms of employee training will occur online. The pandemic has accelerated trends that have been at play for decades, but the advances in technology and video quality have shown that in-person training might not always be required if asynchronous online training can be deployed. As artificial intelligence and machine learning improve over the next 20 years, chatbots embedded in the virtual learning environment can personalize the learning experience for employees. This same technology can be embedded in virtual reality training to give users real-time performance feedback to enhance the efficacy of training.

Recall that some jobs will not be easily replaced by the technologies associated with the *Fourth Industrial Revolution*. Construction, the skilled trades, and many jobs associated with technology development and maintenance will continue to exist. Yet these jobs will surely need to utilize technologies that will be networked together in the Internet of Things. This means that performance management and training will be supplemented by artificial intelligence and machine learning in these jobs. Process improvements uncovered by algorithms that crawl through performance data will make these employees in these traditional jobs more efficient in their work. What is also likely is that jobs will become displaced by the coming wave of the *Fourth Industrial Revolution* – think about those accountants – but the total elimination of those jobs isn't likely. Rather, companies will need fewer employees in those jobs. The scarcity of jobs will highlight the need for finding truly exceptional or high-skilled employees in those jobs. It will be the algorithms that find those employees and the gamification of some selection systems that will help companies choose who will receive the job offer.

Over the next 20 years, human resources professionals will both operate their systems as if economic conditions are good while also running their systems like economic conditions are less than optimal. This will require some dexterity – and strategic nuance – to handle the volume of actions required to operate the people functions within companies that are simultaneously eliminating or dramatically reducing jobs while rapidly expanding staffing, performance management, and training functions for jobs that might not even exist in 2020 plus the kind of jobs that have been around for centuries in the skilled trades. As we peer ahead 50 years into the future of the *Fourth Industrial Revolution* and how that will impact human resources management, societal impacts will be greater as technological advancements accelerate.

6

THE NEXT GENERATION

By the year 2070, the world will be another generation into the *Fourth Industrial Revolution* from where the previous chapter concluded. Whenever humans predict how quickly technology will increase, they seldom prove correct. In previous chapters, we have stated that automation, artificial intelligence, and machine learning capabilities will double within every two decades. Connectivity of machines in the Internet of Things will double every four years. Historically, however, estimates of advancements of technologies often underestimate just how quickly technological advancements improve. For instance, in the 1980s, it was predicted that the connectivity of the Internet and the information it carried would double approximately every three years. Instead, that technology exponentially advanced to the point where the information contained on the Internet is soon predicted to double every 12 hours. So, while we currently think that the technologies associated with the *Fourth Industrial Revolution* will advance in the years stated above, it is likely that the reinforcing cycle of investment, research, and advancement will quicken the rate of change of technologies like automation, artificial intelligence, and machine learning.

So, where does this leave us by the end of the 2070s? Will the dreams of Hollywood writers and directors come true? Likely not. What we can expect, however, is a world where many of the current work-related tasks will no longer be done by humans. Jobs that exist today that still exist in 50 years from now will see significant reengineering through the facilitation of machines. We are also likely to see fewer of those jobs. It is not that machines will totally displace, for example, all accounting jobs. It is more likely that fewer accountants will exist, and those jobs will rely heavily on algorithms and machines to complete the routine facets of the job. Why hire 20 auditors when two auditors paired with a data analyst can do the same amount of work more efficiently and effectively? We will also see a slew of jobs that do not currently exist.[1]

The generational advancements in technology will not only impact jobs, companies, or organizations but impact the people holding those jobs, who do work in those companies or organizations. The experience of humans will change as their work changes. Companies or organizations will change, and the collective experience of working within those companies or organizations will change. We typically think about how employees experience their working environment in terms of a continuum of experiences bounded on one end by climate and on the other end by culture. Culture describes the deeply held and shared values, beliefs, and norms of behaviors. Climate represents the surface representations of an organization's culture. People often describe climate as how a company *feels*. Employees or even visitors to a company will see signs, symbols, logos, or even pictures that appear throughout a company. Employees will use company-specific language or terminology. They will share stories of past events. They might even wear similar attire or fashion esthetic. The office layout and appearance will also convey the climate. Critically, these surface representations – symbols, photos, language, office layout, and the like – link to deeper held company values, beliefs, and norms of behaviors. For instance, if a company values collaboration, employees will use language to reinforce collaboration. The office layout will feature collaborative space.

As automation, artificial intelligence, and machine learning begin to displace jobs and employees within these companies and as new types of jobs appear in their wake, companies and organizations will, by default, have their cultures and climates change. To make this more complex, consider also that companies and organizations will not uniformly adopt the technologies that will drive these transformations. Company supply chains will likely consist of other companies that are in various states of technological adoption and cultural change. One company on the higher end of the technological adoption will have fewer employees but will perhaps deploy chatbots that interact with employees still operating on the lower end of the technological adoption. Machines will talk to humans. Depending upon the leverage one company has over another in a supply chain, will a company have to invest in new technology because they must to in order to remain a partner in that supply chain? Or will the lower technology company have to actually hire more employees who specifically interact with the intelligent machines of the more technologically advanced company? The rolling disruption of the adoption of technology will not only internally roil companies but also will complicate business-to-business interactions between companies.

Inside of companies and organizations, the generational advances of technology adoption will force changes in company culture and climate. Well-planned and executed change interventions take anywhere between 12 and 18 months to occur. A company will identify objectives and distill those down operational goals to advance the change in a strategic, mission-driven manner. Leadership within the company will constantly communicate what changes will occur, when the changes will occur, how the changes will actually happen, and, importantly, why the changes will need to happen. A good change management plan will have every employee understand how the change will impact him or her. The company will deploy change champions and teams to implement the changes. The company will likely utilize visual dashboards to communicate the progress of change. After the changes occur, the company will continue to utilize resources to help employees adapt to the change. And this is if the company has planned and executed the change in a systematic way. Every company or organization will experience these change events over and over as automation, artificial intelligence, and machine learning advance.

As mentioned, the change will not impact just one organization. The change will ripple through companies in a supply chain. Employees who leave a company due to the changes – whether voluntarily or involuntarily – bring their experiences to their new employers, if they can find new employers. Even employees who survive a company's change and do not have technologies to replace their jobs will consider leaving the company. When you see employees leave a company, you wonder how secure your job is and potentially search for another job. In previous chapters, we have noted that some industries will see more job displacement more quickly as automation, artificial intelligence, and machine learning advance. Displaced employees from those industries will flood into other industries, seeking not just work but also opportunities to transfer their existing knowledge, skills, and abilities to another company in a different industry. This means that both companies and societies will experience rolling shocks of abrupt change resulting from technological advancements.

Early in this book, we explained the importance of work to humans. We also explained the importance of work to societies. Three generations of technological advancement between now and 50 years into the future will result in rapid changes to jobs and companies or organizations. Yet, 50 years in the scope of human history and evolution might as well be a nanosecond. It is not as if you have your job displaced by technology and decide that you will no longer work. Of course, you will seek new opportunities to do work that you find meaningful and personally fulfilling. This is why, people continue to look for work when they lose their jobs or have their companies cease operations. This is also why nations around the world provide temporary assistance to those who lose their jobs.

Which brings us to the impact of such rapid employment change on societies? We can use the current example of the COVID-19 pandemic and recession. In the United States, the government passed relatively temporary employment assistance to the millions of Americans who lost their jobs in a matter of weeks. Countries in Europe provided longer relief to their citizens with higher levels of monetary support than did America. Australia and New Zealand passed strict stay-at-home orders coupled with a near halt of any international travel while simultaneously providing financial relief to their citizens. Entire cities in China endured hard shutdowns of economic activity so that citizens could stay inside to avoid spreading the virus, yet these citizens did not have to worry about evictions from their homes or fear starvation. The Chinese government provided relief for these cities.

Like the uneven global response to the COVID-19 pandemic, the global response to the *Fourth Industrial Revolution* will see uneven societal responses to changes in employment and industries. This includes how government agencies will adapt. Countries with centralized employment insurance processes will likely have already adopted artificial intelligence systems to process unemployment benefit claims. They will likely have already identified citizens within their nations who are most at risk to the disruptions inherent to employment from the adoption of technologies associated with the *Fourth Industrial Revolution*. Using algorithms to find these citizens will allow nations to get ahead of waves of unemployment by targeting job retraining initiatives for those at-risk citizens. Governments will utilize integrated artificial intelligence systems to coordinate unemployment insurance, job search assistance, workforce development through training, and the like. These systems will link with private employers, so that governments can provide seamless assistance to citizens. Highly developed democratic-socialist nations in Europe will likely become early adopters of these technologies, as these nations already provide more substantial social safety net services than other nations around the world.

In nations with less centralized federal government structures, such as those that utilize state, prefecture, or municipality governments to handle economic and workforce response and development services, the adoption of artificial intelligence to meet citizens' needs will be less coordinated. For instance, in the United States, individual states vary in how they assist citizens who suffer job displacement during economic shocks. The federal government sets guidelines, but each state differentially administers benefits. States utilize different enterprise resource planning systems to coordinate government-wide processes, which allows for communication gaps between state-to-state systems. That is, as each state utilizes different technology, the machines will not always be able to converse error-free.

These issues all become increasingly important as automation, artificial intelligence, and machine learning accelerate and displace increasingly larger numbers of jobs and employees. The great sorting out of people, jobs, and industries as those technologies become more dominant will cause multiple waves of unemployment and reemployment. How governments respond to these large employment disruptions and the related economic shocks will determine how destabilizing the *Fourth Industrial Revolution* will be to societies. Nations with governments that also adopt the technologies and use those to integrate with businesses will more smoothly provide assistance to citizens. Nations with less federal coordination and adoption of those technologies will certainly struggle to respond to the likely cycles of disruption of employment and industries. Whereas more advanced governments can get ahead of the cycles to better plan responses that will help their citizens, less advanced governments will become more reactive to the changes. This will likely exacerbate the disruptions from the private sector and amplify the chaos that typically follows large-scale economic shocks that affect employment levels in a nation.

The interface between government and employment, even workforce development, obviously impacts the field of human resources. Automated health and safety plans along with reporting of workplace incidences will occur in near real time. As companies transition workforces in response to technological advances, layoffs and employee separations will immediately be reported through automated systems. Diversity, equity, and inclusion issues, including harassment, hostile environment, discrimination, and the like, will also immediately be reported to the appropriate government agencies. These types of automated processes will again happen unevenly across nations as governments adopt the same technologies as companies. Government will also have the ability to publicly make these types of processes and reports available to citizens and other companies and organizations.

Governments and companies will have to navigate the ethical and legal issues inherent in making these types of data publicly available. Will employees have their employment histories, which could potentially contain disciplinary data, made available for all to see? Will organizations and companies have their employee-related data – harassment, discrimination, and the like – made available for all to see? The granularity of data will give insights into the inner workings of companies that we do not currently have, either by design, the lack of data, or legal requirements.

The field of human resources will also experience disruption with the adoption of new technologies. By 2070, companies will have perfected their capabilities to track employee performance. Wearable technology, data from computers, apps, and smartphones, digital data from cameras, customer surveys, productivity data, sales information, and the like will document almost every facet of employee performance. Algorithms, data visualization dashboards, and real-time performance feedback from bots and machines tracking individual employee performance will provide employees with immediate performance feedback. Just like employees in other careers and industries, human resources professionals will see much of their work automated or replaced with artificial intelligence and machine learning capabilities. An employee's history of performance, meticulously captured and analyzed by machines, will help determine which employees keep their jobs and which employees have their jobs replaced by machines. After all, like auditing professionals in accounting, companies will have no need to hire 10 recruiters when two recruiters paired with a data analyst can accomplish the work more efficiently and with fewer mistakes.

This will play out overall disciplines within human resources. If in 2020 almost 670,000 people work in human resources in the United States alone, machines will replace the vast majority of those employees. By 2070, compensation analysis will occur by artificial intelligence applications. Machines will also collect job information for work analysis purposes and allow for changes in job descriptions that then tie into other facets of human resources. Machines will scrape data from Internet sources to help establish pay benchmarks for jobs in the market while also running analyses to determine internal pay rates based on compensable factors. Recruiting will require far fewer employees to execute. Chatbots will answer questions, whether through the Internet or via telephone. As hologram technology improves, those same chatbots will hold virtual conversations with potential applicants during screening calls. If you doubt this technological development, movie fans of the Star Wars movie franchise can point to scenes in the 2016 film *Rogue One* of long deceased actors having their voices and likenesses brought back to life more than 20 years after an actor's death. Employee personality testing, like compensation analysis, will not need human intervention. Algorithms will provide real-time staffing adjustments. As machine learning improves, the need for training specialists will decrease. Algorithms will detect skill gaps in employee performance and identify possible training solutions. Even training manuals will be drafted by artificial intelligence programs. Some aspects of training will be completed by chatbots embedded in holograms. Earlier in this book, we described the process of linking all human resources functions together to create high-performing work systems. Data, algorithms, and other artificial intelligence and machine learning applications will by and large integrate human resources functions across the company. Humans, however, will still need to help link those functions to the company mission. Again, not all human resources professionals will see their jobs displaced.

We have yet to discuss an industry that will require massive overhaul in response to the *Fourth Industrial Revolution* but will be integral in preparing future generations for the revolution. In fact, this industry has been at the forefront of creating the revolution: Higher Education. Academic institutions across the globe conduct research on automation, artificial intelligence, and machine learning. Academicians advance this basic research into new technological applications, which become the basic prototypes that get developed and refined before entering the business market as a product. It is not just companies conducting this research. For example, students taking a course at Georgia Institute of Technology did not know that their teaching assistant was, in fact, a chatbot.[2] A consortium of German universities and technology companies have partnered to create Cyber Valley, which is a hub of research and development around artificial intelligence and machine learning to rival the work done in the Silicon Valley in California.[3] A South Korean university caused an international stir when it was revealed that a robotics and artificial intelligence lab was partnering with a weapons company to develop so-called "killer robots."[4] Strathmore University in Nigeria created @iLabAfrica to spur artificial intelligence and machine learning technology that could be utilized in business settings, such as connecting job seekers and employment opportunities.[5] The University of Sydney developed a chatbot to answer questions that students and parents asked about COVID-19.[6]

Much like every other industry, higher education will see its own research on and creation of robots, algorithms, and smart machines cannibalize parts of its workforce. How many professors or instructors do higher education institutions require to deliver instruction to students? How many librarians or IT help desk employees do universities need to deliver service to students? How many admissions officers will be needed to recruit students? How many academic counselors or advisors will colleges need to help students progress through their programs of study? How many cafeteria employees or groundskeepers will be required to feed students or keep a campus looking kept? A favorite of all university denizens, how many parking meter officers will be needed to check meters or parking tags?

Technology will impact all of these facets of college life. Fewer professors will be needed to deliver instruction as online education system, ushered in by the Covid-19 pandemic, improve and become perfected. Professors can record lectures. Algorithms can grade exams and term papers. Chatbots can respond to student questions. This can be replicated over and over to reach more students without compromising the quality of the instruction. After all, it will be humans who program the machines to do this work, at least until the machines create the deep neural networks that indicate machine learning. Like the delivery of instruction, technology will provide the other services typically found on a college campus. Robots in cafeterias will both cook and serve food. Self-service kiosks will replace check-out attendees. Admissions officers, like their recruiting counterparts in other industries, will see technology reduce their employment ranks. Algorithms will target potential applicants and deliver specialized messaging to those prospective students. Chatbots will respond to questions. Holograms with chatbot capabilities can give campus tours. Smart lawn machines will tend to campus grounds, as computers will control irrigation and fertilizer to make sure the grass on the academic quad looks as beautiful as it ever has. Networks of cameras with smart technology will make sure that you receive a parking ticket when you forget to use your smartphone to pay for more time at the meter.

At this point, you might be asking yourself, "If robots and machines will take over large segments of an economy including higher education, what is the purpose of even going to college?". This, of course, is a natural and valid question. We will later explore a world where large portions of any country's population might have limited employment opportunities, but here we offer a hint of why a future of robots and intelligent machines will still include higher education. First, technology will not displace all industries and jobs. As we have previously described, many current industries and jobs will persist well into the future and certainly beyond 2070. These jobs, while perhaps not needing the same supply of able and educated workers, will continue to need an educated workforce. Second, even in the *Fourth Industrial Revolution*, new jobs and industries will be created. Technical jobs supporting the neural networks developed from artificial intelligence will be created, as will jobs related to personal care and green technology.[7] Interestingly, a future of robots and machines will place a premium on jobs requiring not just technical skills but also demand more person-to-person skills.

Higher education, of course, is for many people the end of an educational system that begins much earlier in a learner's life and spans a far longer period of that learner's life than higher education. Technological changes will not just impact institutions of higher education but will impact primary and secondary educational systems. Science, technology, engineering, and math – acronymed STEM disciplines – will receive far more educational attention in primary and secondary education around the world. In the year 2020, these disciplines already receive quite a bit of attention; but by 2070, young learners will become more facile with STEM-related expertise at younger ages. Robotics, coding, engineering, and the like will be taught at earlier ages than we might see now. However, recall that while automation, artificial intelligence, and machine learning will displace millions of jobs and cause the extinction of entire industries, many jobs and industries will remain quite intact far into the future. The skilled and construction trades, for instance, will likely see little displacement in the *Fourth Industrial Revolution*; yet even those trades will require education in the STEM disciplines.

As we mentioned earlier in this chapter, a fundamental paradox of the *Fourth industrial Revolution* will emerge. On one hand, automation, artificial intelligence, and machine learning will affect almost every facet of human life. Technology will displace jobs and industries in cyclical waves that will cause conflict and strife within societies. Humans will continue to seek value and meaning in their lives related to work, yet it is likely that more jobs will be displaced than added during the *Fourth Industrial Revolution*. On the other hand, however, human interaction will be more valued as societies embrace more technology.

Let us use the example of dining at a restaurant. By 2070, it is likely that most fast food or cafeteria-style restaurants will be almost entirely staffed by artificially intelligent machines that possess singular intelligence. That is, the machine will be self-aware and no longer require human intervention to learn via coding. The machines will handle the logistics of operating the restaurant, from purchasing ingredients and maintaining inventory to washing used dishes and utensils to cleaning tables and floors after diners eat. It is likely in the next 50 years that machines will be able to cook-to-order myriad meals in ways that most diners will not know that their meal has been cooked by a robot. Ordering food, serving food, and paying for the meal will happen without human touch. Machines will make eating out more efficient and likely more cost effective for dining patrons without sacrificing the quality of the meal. In fact, this type of food production might be healthier, as the data-driven processes behind this type food production and service will undoubtedly find healthier ingredient and cooking alternatives than are available in today's world.

However, patrons sometimes desire to have an experience while dining out, and this is where human interaction will take precedence over the cheap and efficient experience of artificially intelligent dining. Fine dining restaurants will still cater to patrons who seek a personalized dining experience. Human chefs, while likely armed with machine help, will still create handcrafted meals. Servers and hosts will still provide personalized greetings and service touches. Handcrafted spirits and drinks will still be produced by bartenders who know their customers. Car parking valets and restaurant attendants will make patrons' arrivals and departures personalized experiences. While the machine-enabled world of fast food or cafeteria-style dining will be cost effective, patrons will pay a premium for the personalized experiences of fine dining.

Thus, an interesting dynamic will occur in many service-related industries that exist in 2020 and will exist in 2070. Consumers will have choices between efficient and cost-effective services that automation, artificial intelligence, and machine learning will enable and more costly highly personalized service experiences that rely on human touch. Again, the *Fourth Industrial Revolution* will likely not displace all jobs in a specific industry as it will greatly reduce the number of employees required in those jobs and industries.

For human resources management professionals, this means that they will essentially operate two distinct types of human resources systems. One system will operate at the strategic level where humans will make decisions about how to deploy automation, artificial intelligence, and machine learning technologies. Fewer human resources professionals will be required for this type of system. Machines will handle much of the operational work that human resources professionals currently conduct – from recruiting and selection to training and performance management. The second system, however, will still require quite a significant piece of human intervention. If you operate a fine dining restaurant that caters to patrons who are willing to spend a premium on the experience of dining, you will still likely use artificial intelligence and machine learning to help you make decisions around recruiting, selection, training, and performance management; but, you will still likely spend quite a bit of time performing the operational work of those human resources functions. Like the dining experience your restaurant creates though human connection, your human resource management work will similarly require human connection to help the restaurant meet its mission.

This bifurcation of human resources management work will create challenges. Companies must understand the requirements of its business; moreover, companies must have a firm grasp on its mission and market. Who are they? Who do they serve? Who are their customers? A single organization or company might serve multiple markets with multiple products. Some of those products will serve markets that automation, artificial intelligence, and machine learning technologies can handle more efficiently and cost-effectively. Some of those products will serve markets, however, that require human-to-human interaction. Human resources management professionals and functions must be able to accommodate a spectrum of work that can be totally done via machine through work that is still mostly done by humans. That is, human resources management as a field will require more agility than it perhaps does now. It will also require a mindset that understands that machines and humans are not mutually exclusive choices for companies or organizations.

Rather, there will be human resources management solutions that span a continuum from machines to humans.

Over the next 50 years, automation, artificial intelligence, and machine learning will increase in velocity. Workforces will contract and expand in cycles that will create stress on employees, companies, and societies. Some jobs and industries will cease to exist, while others will significantly change as technologies advance. Human resources management professionals will have to be adept in using the same technologies that will cause disruptions across industries – including their own – but also maintain knowledge of how to do human resources work in a very human way. Human resources professionals will have to understand that even amid technological advances, strategic decisions around adopting and using those technologies must be made by humans. In the next 50 years, human resources professionals will be awash in data, from recruiting and selection data to performance management data. Yet, these professionals must always remember that these data serve to inform human decisions, not replace human decisions. That paradox of more technology but more human interaction will continue to be important well into the next generation of the *Fourth Industrial Revolution*.

7

A CENTURY OF STRESS HEADED INTO THE NEXT CENTURY

From a change perspective, the current century will *feel* like no other century in recorded history. This sounds hyperbolic, and perhaps it is. Consider, however, the cumulative effect of what will have occurred. Instantaneous, real-time communication via the integration of traditional media – newspapers, broadcast journalism – and citizen journalism and social media tweets, Facebook posts, uploads from citizens' phones, and constant on-air reporting break news within seconds of an event occurring. The technologies of the *Fourth Industrial Revolution* will unevenly disrupt jobs, industries, economies, and societies across the globe. Millions of years of human evolution have imbued within our species the importance of work in defining who we are, yet machines will displace so much human work over a brief hundred-year time period. Climate change and a new era of global pandemics will roil nations across the globe and be reported in real time. New industries will emerge while traditional industries will wane and, for some, cease to exist. It will be a lot for humans to take in over such a brief period of time, and it will be broadcasted live and in real-time across phones, tablets, wearable technology, television screens, and radio streaming services.

We deliberately use the word *feel* when describing the likely unprecedented changes occurring over the twenty-first century into the twenty-second century. History, of course, teaches us that every century contains advancements and events that force species to adapt. The twentieth century contained two world wars that fundamentally altered the world. Nineteenth century Victorian notions of chivalry and class were obliterated in the muddy trenches and front lines of places like Verdun, Ypres, and the Argonne Forest. Tanks, weaponized airplanes, and gruesome new weapons were all invented and deployed to break through miles of trenches and barbed wire. The Spanish flu pandemic swept across the war-torn world, killing more people than the Great War did. The redrawn post–World War I boundaries created new nations in the Middle East, divvying up the spoils of war from a collapsed trio of axis nations and seeding a deep discontent among some in the defeated nations. Russia experienced a revolution that saw the creation of a new type of government that would become an ideological and later military competitor to democratic nations around the world. A postwar economic boom ended in the deepest economic depression that conspired to create an environment where previous resentments and technological advances led to a second world war. The invention of the atomic bomb formally ended World War II, which led to a decade of relative global peace and prosperity. Weary of world conflagrations but eager to expand influence, the world's two post–World War II powers engaged in a global cold war. Two long and costly wars in Asia and a missile crisis in the Caribbean kept the world on edge as technological innovations, many of which were developed during the century's wars, rapidly spread across the globe. As the end of the twentieth century approached, global economies built on services, and knowledge work dominated the globe and set the necessary conditions for the *Fourth Industrial Revolution*.

For most of us reading this book, that brief history of the twentieth century exists in history books. Even for those of us alive during an objectively tumultuous 100-year time span, many of these events happen in far-off locations that we could only read about weeks or months after events occurred. A global consciousness did not exist during the twentieth century that now exists in the twenty-first century. The net effect of this global consciousness is that events, even fleeting events, feel more pressing or urgent. It is this feeling of time that will make the twenty-first century *feel* different than previous centuries.

You can think about time in two different ways. For many of us in Western societies, we typically only think about time in a linear sense. Sometimes referred to as clock time, linear time refers to the actual marking of measured time. Our minutes have 60 seconds. Our hours have 60 minutes. Our days have 24 hours and so on to months, years, decades, and centuries. We live our days according to time. We schedule events and meetings based on specific markers of clock time. We organize our work into manageable chunks of time. We plan our company strategy based upon calendar years that include mandatory financial reporting deadlines. This type of linear or clock time provides structure to many of our lives. We look backwards into our past and forward into our futures using the structure of linear time. This book itself is organized, in part, around linear time.

Yet, we also experience time in a fundamentally different way that is completely detached from linear time. Psychological time refers to how we feel about the passage of time. Sometimes, an hour can feel like a few minutes. Sometimes, an hour can feel like a day. For instance, you have probably heard of the phrase "employee engagement." Your work probably surveys its employees in an attempt to understand how engaged the workforce is. Engagement contains three components: vigor, dedication, and absorption. You can think of vigor as feeling energized and dedicated as committed to whatever task you are completing. Absorption occurs when you get lost in your work or experience. When you enter a state of absorption, you will spend hours on your work and lose track of linear time. Hours will fly by without you noticing it. You will tell your coworkers that it felt like you had only worked for an hour while the actual clock time said you had worked a full day. Absorption gets to this idea of psychological time. In a sense, psychological time renders linear time moot. While humans can independently experience both linear and psychological time, they can also concurrently experience them.

What do linear and psychological time have to do with our statement about the twenty-first century *feeling* like no other time period? Let us use the COVID-19 pandemic as an example. At the start of the pandemic when nations began to shut down their economies and quarantining their populations, many people reported the feeling that time stood still or seemed to last forever. The governor of New York famously began his daily public briefings by reminding citizens what day of the week it was. People had lost all sense of linear time, but psychologically they felt that time was standing still. Six months into the pandemic people began reporting the opposite: time appeared to be flying by. The interaction between linear and psychological time added to the general confusion many people felt around the world as the pandemic and its global effects persisted into the end of 2020. Because technology has enabled a global consciousness around events and crises, the people across the planet shared similar experiences as new events in the pandemic unfolded.

The net effect of a global crisis combined with technological advancements in how humans communicate and consume news in real time is increased stress. Stress refers to any demand placed on you to which you must respond. Stressors can take the form of physical, cognitive, emotional, or relational stimuli. When you experience stress, you must dedicate your resources to meet the demands of the stressor. Resources can take the form of material, emotional, physical, or relational responses. For instance, your supervisor can unexpectedly ask you to perform a task that has a short turnaround time. This stress places a demand on you that will need to dedicate resources to in order to complete the task. Consider the resources you will have to muster to meet this new demand. You will divert cognitive resources by shifting your other work to prioritize the urgent task. You will divert relationship resources by asking your coworkers to perhaps shift some of your existing work to them. You will divert physical resources to complete the task, perhaps working well into the night. You will divert emotional resources – anger, fear, hope, happiness – to meet the new demands placed on you.

Unfortunately, we have finite resources to meet the demands of our lives. Consider this extended metaphor. Your resources can fill a bucket, and each day the level of the resources in your bucket will vary. Each day you wake up, you spend the rest of your day slowly pouring out your resources to meet the demands of your life. Think of all of the decisions you make between waking up and leaving your house for work – what to eat, what to wear, what time to leave? Those represent small demands that require very few resources to pour from your bucket. But larger demands likely await you during the day. What relationships do you have to navigate, both personal and professional? What responsibilities do you have both inside and outside of work? How much effort – cognitive, physical, and emotional – do you have to exert to complete your work? How well do you take care of your physical and mental well-being? Do you eat and sleep well? You spend your day emptying your resource bucket, and you also spend quite a bit of time each day trying to gain more resources. Your work provides you with compensation that you use to further the goals of your life. You rely upon friends, family, and coworkers to provide much needed support. Over and over each day, you expend resources to meet the demands of your life but look for opportunities to replenish your bucket. Weekends and vacation represent opportunities to replenish your resource bucket as you head back to work.

This is the daily cycle of stress and coping that you seldom think about, as having to even think about it places a demand on your resources. It is when our resource bucket gets depleted that we begin to experience more dangerous outcomes. When we experience stress that we can no longer mitigate by expending our resources, we develop burnout. Burnout consists of three components: withdrawal, reduced self-efficacy, and emotional exhaustion. Withdrawal describes the tendency to reduce contact with others or pull back from activities that we might normally do. Reduced self-efficacy refers to the feeling that we can no longer successfully complete tasks or do things what we previously felt confident in completing or doing. Emotional exhaustion is that feeling that you cannot muster the energy to respond to stressors. Of the three components, emotional exhaustion is considered the leading edge of burnout. When your alarm goes off in the morning and you immediately sigh or say to yourself, "I just can't today," that is emotional exhaustion. It means that your resource bucket is empty, and you cannot meet the demands of the day. Once emotional exhaustion hits, you will begin to doubt yourself in almost every facet of your life. You will also begin to withdraw from relationships and activities; simply, you do have the resources to do the activities that you would normally do. You will enter the psychological state of burnout, and the consequences of burnout are significant. Your job satisfaction, commitment, and performance will decrease, which will further expose you to potential crises – you could lose your job. Your relationships will suffer, as you enter preservation mode and prioritize only activities and relationships that will add to your resources instead of draining them. Your health will decline, both emotionally and physically. Burnout is associated with depression and mental health crises. Burnout is associated with weight gain, poor heart health, poor immune responses to colds and flus, and self-harm behaviors. It is common that once someone enters burnout that their inability to muster resources to meet the demands of life will spiral into further losses. Not only will poor job outcomes occur, but poor health and relationship outcomes will occur. Burnout, holistically speaking, is a brutal psychological state to experience.

In the context of the *Fourth Industrial Revolution*, the velocity of change will increase as technological advancements ripple through jobs, companies, industries, and economies. From an employee or company perspective, think of these changes as shocks. Employees will lose their jobs to machines, and employees will have to muster the resources to meet the demands of unemployment and job search while having fewer resources to bring to bear to meet these demands. Similarly, companies will experience disruptive shocks as employees exit or as the companies' products are no longer needed at the levels that will sustain companies' financial well-being. Mergers and acquisitions will increase as better leveraged companies seek to purchase competitors or complementary companies, triggering more shocks to employees and companies. As we see during recessions and financial shocks, unemployment rises, and governments must intervene. Otherwise, the fabric of nations falls apart, and mass emigration or violence typically ensues. The twenty-first century will see these shocks and societal responses over and over as the technologies spurring the *Fourth Industrial Revolution* are fully implemented and displace entire industries. This is the stress to which we refer at the start of this chapter, and it will occur as people around the world watch in real time wondering how this will affect their lives and their nations – creating stress despite the absence of the events in their own countries. The repeated and globally broadcast crises will feel constant, and the crises simultaneously feel like they last forever but happen quickly in succession, which will only add to the stress we will feel.

For human resources professionals, the fields' experience in change management and staffing will position its professionals well in dealing with the cycles of technological adoption–job displacement–adjustment that will ripple through large swaths of the planet over the twenty-first century. It is also important to remember that human resources structures already exist in the interface between societies and their governments and how human resources operates. In the previous chapter, we discussed how companies will adopt in their human resources functions, the very technologies that will be displacing employees in the *Fourth Industrial Revolution*. The more integrated the reporting systems between companies and governments, the timelier and efficiently companies will adapt with their human resources functions to employment assistance and workforce development programs that governments will likely offer in the transition to technologies like automation, artificial intelligence, and human resources. By the twenty-second century, these public–private interfaces will be highly coordinated, likely due to artificial intelligence algorithms that will help bridge reporting gaps between governments and companies or organizations.

Human resources professionals that work in areas of change and transformation will become in demand throughout the remainder of the twenty-first century and into the twenty-second century. These professionals will utilize integrated human resources functions and the data that those functions collect through myriad technological devices – phones, tablets, computers, wearable technology, video technology – to iden-tify problem areas in change management interventions. This is where humans will provide value – in the linkage of functional-level data to strategic initiatives. The machines will not set company strategy; humans will. While many companies might utilize more intelligent machines than humans to meet companies' missions, human assets will still provide considerable value to companies. It will be the change management specialists that will utilize data and develop change management plans that address the machine and human sides of organizational transformation. Personalized and timely communication will still be key in transformation interventions. Working with humans and machines to meet project management deadlines will remain important. It is in the change management areas of human resources that we will likely see the true interface between machines and humans functioning to help companies meet their missions.

Human resources professionals in the staffing function of companies will also be well positioned to deal with employment shocks and very different labor markets than we saw in the twenty-first century. Staffing professionals might have fewer jobs requiring humans to staff, recruit, and select; but finding the right mix of humans and machines to meet company goals or needs while also finding the best fitting human employees will be increasingly difficult. On the staffing mix side of the job, algorithms will certainly provide optimized staffing mixes to complete work. Staffing specialists will have more data about myriad variables at their fingertips when trying to understand the optimal mix of employees and machines. Yet, human discretion will still be key. All data contain error, even if algorithms can provide statistical adjustments for error. Consider the retail industry during the holiday season. By the twenty-second century, robots and machines will be common in retail stores around the globe. While some retail shops might become robot-only businesses, others will utilize a mix of robots and humans. Staffing professionals will need to determine where to deploy robots and humans to maximize the customer experience. They will base their decisions on value provided. In some areas of a retail store, robots will provide the most value – perhaps in the ordering, loading, stocking, and inventory areas of the store. Kiosks and self-help technologies that deploy chatbots and virtual or hologram assistants will help customers in specific areas of the retail shop. However, some areas will still require human connection – perhaps in high-end product sections of the retail space.

Consider the challenge for staffing professionals at this juncture. Data and algorithms will help in the decision-making process, but a human will need to understand the exact points at which to deploy humans in order to maximize the value of the experience to shoppers. Consider also the challenge in actually finding the best fitting employee to fill these high-value jobs. In a world where machines will increasingly displace humans in routine, easily automated jobs, how do staffing professionals actually find human employees? By the twenty-second century, machines will capture data on almost every facet of human life starting at very young ages. Machines will have access to educational performance, skill development, emotional growth and maturity, job performance, health, previous compensation, social and professional reputation, social media posts and interactions, and myriad other variables associated with human life. How will staffing professionals sift through all of these data? Obviously, machines and algorithms will help find the needles in the massive labor haystacks, but human intervention will still need to occur in the hiring process – although perhaps much later in the process than it does in the twenty-first century. To add to the complexity in this situation, staffing professionals will have true global labor markets to sift through in order to find the best fitting employees for specific jobs that maximize value to the customer. With fewer jobs, more applicants, and jobs requiring finely tuned knowledge, skills, and abilities, the relatively fewer jobs that humans will fill will be highly compensated jobs. Supply and demand in labor markets will not go away in the twenty-second century.

Performance management in the twenty-second century will become more instantaneous and developmental for the likely smaller workforces in nations that are further along in the adoption of automation, artificial intelligence, and machine learning technologies. Technology will allow for the collection of employee performance from the start of an employee's career. Instead of a resume or curriculum vitae, an employee will present his or her history of performance, skills acquisition and development, educational or professional degrees or certifications, and any other relevant information to potential employers, likely through similar platforms that currently exist such as LinkedIn or other websites. These types of platforms with historical data on each applicant will also make it easier for companies to proactively recruit or poach high-skilled and in-demand employees.

Human resource professionals will continue to utilize all-encompassing data collection techniques to conduct work analysis. As machines and employees conduct work, the performance data kicked off from employees will also help identify inefficiencies in process flows or emerging tasks for jobs or needed employee skills to complete a job. For the machines, their ability to learn without human intervention will make these types of processes seamless. Work analysis will also help identify skill gaps that training interventions can close. Instead of conducting labor-intensive experiments to understand the best training delivery methods, algorithms will run simulations using real performance data from employees. Simulations, virtual or otherwise, will be the norm for all training situations, even in retail. Why conduct any training interventions on the job when machines can create high fidelity simulations to train employees? Gone will be the days of on-the-job training or other high-risk training interventions that expose job novices to risk of failure in ways that will harm the trainee, company, or customers? The *Fourth Industrial Revolution* will allow for the full integration of human resources management systems, and human decision-makers will deploy optimal human or machine capital to help companies meet their missions.

Like the work environments of the twenty-first century, human resources professionals will also oversee the systems related to employee well-being. Earlier in this chapter, we discussed how the twenty-first century will be the most stressful time period for humans. Many organizations today utilize various techniques to help reduce employee stress. This will continue well into the twenty-second century as employees, even in smaller workforces, will add considerable value to organizations. While technologies will help staffing specialists proactively find the best fitting employee for every position, employee turnover will continue to disrupt organizations and be something that organizations will always look to reduce. Access to data about employees will help identify indicators of employee well-being. Wearable technology, patterns in work behaviors, biomedical markers, and the like give human resources professionals data to analyze about employee well-being. Forget about monthly employee surveys. By the twenty-second century, data proxies for employee general work attitudes, health, and well-being will exist, and algorithms will identify patterns in employee well-being that will allow for early interventions. This will allow human resources professionals to take on more care roles within the company to personally help employees live happier and healthier lifestyles. Healthy workers are productive workers.

There is a final issue to consider about the future work environment related to an integrated human resources management system that uses data and machines to help optimize employee performance: employee retention. To this point in the chapter, we have predicted a future where data and algorithms identify patterns in employee behaviors and attitudes that indicated employee performance, health, and well-being. Like the paradox we described in the last chapter, while technology will displace so much of what we know about humans at work, all of the technology will actually enhance the need for human interaction even from a human resource perspective. Employees remain with and leave jobs for different reasons. Often, the primary determinant of why employees remain or leave a job is the relationship an employee has with his or her boss. We do not foresee a work environment in which employees directly report to machines. We do believe, however, that fewer employees in workplaces will mean fewer employees will report to a supervisor. If that ideal span of control – the number of direct reports to a single supervisor – is less than seven employees per manager, that ratio will be smaller in future workplaces. This means that the relationship between supervisors and subordinates will become even more crucial than it already is. Again, data and algorithms can help to ensure better matches between supervisors and subordinates when new employees join a company or organization. However, relationship management will still come down to the quality of person-to-person interactions.

Virtual management assistants and virtual reality programs will surely help train managers and guide their own performance when it comes to managing subordinates, yet conflict is a permanent feature of human behavior. Data and algorithms will certainly detect patterns in supervisor and subordinate attitudes and behaviors indicative of emerging conflict, and companies will be fortunate for early warning systems that can identify opportunities for early conflict resolution interventions. Turnover will still occur, and it will still cost companies to replace employees.

In an interconnected world where recruiters can identify best-fitting employees by using algorithms to crawl through data and where there will be a glut of employees relative to available jobs, the competition between companies for employee talent will be fierce. Socializing employees into any organization will still require months – currently it takes between 12 and 18 months for employees to fully onboard and understand a company's culture and whether or not they fit into that culture. Competitors for talent will capitalize on any poor hiring decisions in attempts to poach employees from other companies. Performance management systems inside of companies will also make it more likely that higher performing employees remain at a company, as poorer performing employees – even those benefitting from real-time performance management and virtual training opportunities – will leave organizations. It is likely that the smaller workforces of the future will consist of the best performing employees. These are attractive and prized employees that competing companies will tirelessly try to recruit away. Just like today, a company's human resources management systems will integrate to create high performing work systems that engender employee commitment. Take care of your employees, and they will take care of the company.

In some ways, this all might seem quite dystopic. Smaller workforces, streams of data tracking every facet of human life, companies using those data to identify issues and intervene early, and machines providing insights into your life about what is best for you. We will describe in later chapters the positive and healthy outcomes of the ongoing *Fourth Industrial Revolution*, but before we do, we will first need to describe some likely changes to the composition of workforces that will bring with its dramatic effects on society. What we have described in this chapter might only apply to a small but vital segment of any nation's workforce. What about the rest of the workforce?

8

SERVING MULTIPLE SEGMENTS
OF THE POPULATION

We cannot predict with certainty that our version of the future of jobs, companies, industries, and societies will come to pass. We have based our thinking on current technological trends associated with automation, artificial intelligence, and machine learning and what these trends might mean for employees, companies, and societies. We know, like previous industrial revolutions, that jobs will be displaced as companies adopt new technologies. We know that as jobs get disrupted that displaced employees must enter a labor market that will include other people displaced from jobs due to the same technological shift. We know that governments and societies will respond to the increased size of the labor market due to unemployment. Citizens will receive unemployment benefits and government-backed programs to reskill and deploy their skills back into different jobs. Indeed, new jobs in new fields will absorb people back into the workforce. Economies will recover and stability will return. What we have explored to this point in the book is how the field of human resources management will respond to this cycle as the technologies of

the Fourth Industrial Revolution permanently displace
employees from jobs and industries while shrinking the size of
workforces in industries that remain as new industries come
into existence.

The great unknown about this future is whether or not the
technologies of *the Fourth Industrial Revolution* will limit the
size and growth of workforces in surviving and emerging
industries. The question still remains: will automation, artificial
intelligence, and machine learning immediately displace human
work even in newly created jobs and industries? That is, will
technology remove the need for human work? Perhaps our
view of this future skews toward an extreme of a continuum of
thought on this issue. Some might believe that, like previous
industrial revolutions, an equilibrium exists whereby new jobs
and industries will absorb displaced employees. Jobs go away,
industries collapse, new industries emerge, and new jobs are
created to again balance supply and demand of jobs and
employees. While this version of the future is plausible and,
based on historical precedence, more likely to occur than not,
we find it prudent to explore the possibility that this technological revolution will permanently reduce the need for human
labor. After all, as machines become self-aware and develop
deep neural networks that also connect devices in the Internet
of Things, what futuristic jobs could come into existence that
the machines will not immediately displace?

Recall that not all jobs and industries will collapse.
Machines will replace jobs with highly repetitive facets of
work. Machines will replace jobs that require less autonomy
and independent decision-making. Machines will replace jobs
that do not add value beyond what an intelligence machine
could contribute a lower cost. But also recall the paradox that
as machines remove so much human interaction that human
interaction will become more valuable. Recall also that the
cost of developing and producing machines has to be less than

the cost of attracting, developing, and retaining human employees; otherwise, there is no business case for adopting technologies to ever removing humans from the workforce. So, some industries and jobs – like many in the construction industry and skilled trade fields – will continue to see machines as complementary to the work that humans do.

At the end of 2020, the global workforce contained just under 3.5 billion employees.[1] The world will have undergone an expansion of population from 7.6 billion people to a peak of 9.7 billion people by 2064 but then regress to 8.8 billion people by 2100.[2] If current labor participation rates continue – and they have been quite stabile this century at 65% – the global workforce will consist of 5.7 billion people by 2100, off of a 6.3 billion person high in 2064. This expansion then contraction of population will result from mortality rates associated with the effects of global warming and an expected increase in the frequency of pandemics in the future. Such population booms and busts will cause instability in nations as resources become scarcer. Population decrease also results in natural decreases in economic activity. More people mean more purchasing. Fewer people mean less purchasing. Layer on to the expected growth and collapse of world population, the displacement of people from their work, and, again, the next 100 years will contain quite a bit of instability.

To give a sense of how the number of unemployed people will fluctuate over the next century, consider that at the end of 2020, the global unemployment rate sat at 5.4%.[3] As we mentioned earlier in Chapter 6, economic recessions on average occur every 8 years. Indeed, data from the World Bank reflect the trailing indicator of unemployment to recessions. The Dot.Com recession of the early 2000s saw global unemployment rise to nearly 6.2% before receding to a twenty-first century low of 5.3% in 2008. The Great Recession that started in 2008 saw global unemployment rise to 6%

in 2009 and has steadily decreased to its current level. In Chapter 5, we described the individual and societal effects of unemployment during recessions. As the size of the global workforce rises, increases in unemployment rates will mean commensurately larger numbers of people on unemployment and seeking work. Naturally, having more unemployed members of a society will increase the strain on governments and societies. As populations and economies shrink, societal instability will also increase. However, what might happen with the displacement of jobs and industries due to techno-logical advancements in the Fourth Industrial Revolution is that the displacement of jobs and industries due to technology might not affect economic indicators like gross domestic product. Consider that companies, despite losing employees, will likely remain highly efficient. We should not expect a reduction in work output or production when machines take over for human employees. That is exactly one of the forces driving technological advancement and adoption. The machines cost less and are more efficient at work than are humans. Detangling the effects of unemployment from tech-nological displacement from a nation's overall economic productivity will be challenging for economists and policy makers. Traditionally, we view increased unemployment as decreasing economic demand. Citizens with less money will purchase fewer products and services unless unemployment benefits are robust enough to offset the loss of income.

While this might seem detached from the work of human resources professionals, economic forces, as we have previ-ously discussed, impact the daily work of human resources professionals. Population and workforce growth and decline affect labor markets and available talent. Yet there is another aspect to the adoption of the technologies of the *Fourth Industrial Revolution* that we have yet to explore but is perhaps implied in the discussions we have had in this chapter.

It is likely that 100 years from now, many societies across the planet will have highly segmented workforces. One segment, likely a small segment, will consist of highly technical jobs related to developing, implementing, and maintaining the technologies associated with *the Fourth Industrial Revolution*. Another segment will be familiar to us in the twenty-first century: business services. Companies will still need business services like marketing, finance, accounting, supply chain management, human resources, and the like. Governments will still require workforces, albeit likely smaller than now. Consultants, especially those focusing on the interplay between technology, industry, business functions, and strategy, will still ply their trade across business and industries. Humans will still work in medical and allied-medical professions, as they will in the legal profession. This segment of the workforce will be much smaller in the future than it is currently in many societies, as technology will displace many jobs. These jobs, even in the medical fields, will rely upon robotics and related intelligent technologies to provide value to customers. A third segment of the workforce of the future will consist of skilled and construction trades, high-end retail and care services, and teachers. Robots, artificial intelligence applications, and self-aware machines will help professionals in these professions, but, as we discussed in Chapter 3, machines do not add tremendous value in industries that require high-touch tasks. Plumbers and carpenters will use technology to help plan or diagnose solutions, but the nature of the work will require human touch. Builders and construction professionals will still do most of the work of creating new facilities and homes. Similarly, as customers will increasingly value human touch in some parts of the retail industry, professionals will continue to provide high-touch experiences to diners, customers seeking entertainment, and personal shopping types of experiences. Customers will pay a premium for the added touch of human employees. While fast food and cafeteria-style restaurants or pharmacies or low-cost grocery stores will largely be manned by robots and artificially intelligent applications, high-end shops, restaurants, and grocers will cater to those willing to pay for a personalized experience.

Despite or maybe because of what the world has experienced during the COVID-19 pandemic, educational professionals will continue to thrive in the workforce of the twenty-second century. Technology, as we now have experienced with applications like Zoom and Microsoft Teams, will help educators reach wider audiences. However, as we discussed in Chapter 2, humans are social animals that require in-person interaction with other humans, especially in educational settings. We, of course, will have come to understand the effects of "remote" or "distant" education in the wake of the COVID-19 pandemic, but it does not require a doctorate in developmental psychology to see that children, adolescents, and college students have struggled to learn in a purely remote or virtual educational environment. Social development and educational development occur in tandem even through college. What the COVID-19 pandemic has shown is that educators can create more robust learning environments when they can use technology to supplement not displace instruction. Given the millions of years of evolution that has created modern humans, technological advances cannot so easily roll back our needs for social interaction and how learning is tied to those social interactions.

The idea of care services might sound to our twenty-first-century ears as something related to medical or elder care. Perhaps the idea is not too far off from that but it needs to be seen in a bigger sense. Currently in many societies, if you interact with the medical profession in a hospital or emergency situation, you have likely interacted with professionals that help coordinate your care or who coordinate your care with family members or friends. These types of professionals help explain complex processes and procedures. They help connect patients and their families with other resources or services. They follow up not on medical issues but on issues related to patients' and families' overall well-being. Social workers fit into the idea of a care professional, but in the twenty-second century, as technology has displaced so many jobs and industries, new jobs that are similar to social workers will emerge to help people navigate their lives. This will become clearer as we discuss the last segment of a future workforce – and likely a large segment of the workforce – that has been shaped by automation, artificial intelligence, and machine learning.

At the dawn of the twenty-first century, the idea of a gig worker or the gig economy became common not just in thought but in action. Employees string together a series of contracts or short-term jobs to form their careers, whether out of necessity or choice. The final segment of the future workforce extends this notion of the gig employee. It is likely that through the tumult of the twenty-first century as the *Fourth Industrial Revolution* accelerates and displaces employees, jobs, companies, and industries, a large portion of any society's population will not work in full-time jobs or even have careers in the same sense of how they think about careers in the twenty-first century. There simply will not be enough jobs for humans to work due to the prevalence and sophistication of intelligent machines. This does not mean, however, that millions of years of human evolution will somehow unwind the meaning of work to humans. Humans will still want to work, but for many societies, the opportunities to work in a full-time job will not be readily available nor accessible.

Humans will work predominantly in gig job opportunities, and as we discuss in the final chapter of this book, humans will find other creative outlets to apply their drive to work.

It will be the role of care workers to help facilitate gig job opportunities and avenues for humans to direct their creativity, passion, energy, and skills into opportunities that benefit themselves and their societies. For those of us old enough to remember – or for those who love to delve into 1970s and 1980s American television history – the television series *The Love Boat* aired from 1977 to 1987. The show depicted a cruise ship and its plucky crew, who, through the magic of the Love Boat's itinerary, amenities, and special guests, produced amorous encounters and outcomes among the ship's passengers. One of the characters of *The Love Boat*, was Julie McCoy – played by Lauren Tewes – the ship's Cruise Director. As the Cruise Director, it was Julie's job to plan activities for the ship and for its passengers. Whether specific on-board activities, special meals, special events, off-ship excursions when in port, Julie could develop the best itinerary for every passenger. In the twenty-second century, care workers will be the Julie, Cruise Directors for vast swaths of citizens in many societies.

It is in these societal "care" roles that human resource professionals will add value. Human resources management academics and practitioners have more than a century of experience developing, validating, and utilizing personality and vocational preference tests. The very smart technology applications and algorithms used today to identify best-fitting applicants for jobs and company cultures will in the future apply to helping match gig employees to gig work and other pursuits so that segments of this expanded gig workforce can find meaning in their work and lives. From young ages, citizens will have data about their skills, abilities, and preferences collected, much like today, in government agencies. Citizens will have their educational progress, skills, and knowledge acquisition tracked. Purchasing history, like today through Amazon and Google, will provide lifelong data about citizens' interests. Social media posts about athletic interests or achievements, family milestones and celebrations, and the like will all be tracked and curated. By the time a citizen reaches adulthood, personality, interests, and vocational profiles will exist to help place specific citizens into gig or creative outlets to direct their behaviors into meaningful and productive work or activities.

Much like vertically and horizontally integrating human resources management systems to create high-performing work systems that elicit reciprocal employee and organizational commitment to increase performance and retention, the same thinking will apply to societies. Governments must identify ways to keep citizens engaged and productive, lest discontent and alienation settle into populations. Such negative feelings spread like viruses through populations and lead to societal chaos. Recall again the precipitating economic conditions that triggered two world wars and multiple societal revolutions in the twentieth century. Because the twenty-first century will likely feature more economic boom and bust cycles – the natural economic expansions and contractions coupled with the technological-driven displacement of employees, jobs, and industries – governments will need to shift attention to ramifications of a large segment of workforces that are essentially permanent gig employees; and potentially gig citizens.

You might at this point wonder how the sorting of citizens into these different workforce segmentations will occur. It likely will begin before a citizen is born, as data about previous generations become digitized and organized into linear family histories around personality, values, interests, vocations, and the like. Psychologists have long known that personality traits and individual differences – like intelligence – are inheritable.[4] Values, beliefs, and interests have strong social learning components, whereby parents teach their offspring these structures and become role models for their offspring to emulate.[5] In terms of vocational preferences, look no further than the apprentice systems from the Middle Ages for the power of passing vocations from family members to family members. One of the authors of this book has a family surname that connotes the occupation of wheelmaking; the other is from a group of herders. Also consider all of the data currently tracked on your smartphone, social media, and purchasing information, which means that your data become linked to the data about your family members and even, potentially, your yet-to-be-born offspring.

The role of education will continue to the data collection around individuals and their eventual sorting into the workforce segments we've described. Currently in many nations, achievement and progression tests measure students' propensity for academic success and vocational interests. Students who demonstrate success and interest in science, technology, engineering, and math disciplines are funneled into educational programs to develop those skills and interests. These programs could be academic and theoretical or practitioner focused. It is not uncommon in many parts of the world today for mid-adolescent aged students to receive education on a "college" or "university" track, while other similar-aged students are tracked into "vocational" or "technical" training. The availability of big data to supplement this type of academic system will act as a strong sorting mechanism into the different workforces, much like it already does today. In other nations, such as the United States, this type of educational process does not exist; in fact, that nation's cultural norms are, at least now, anathema to such "government-led" educational interventions. The types of educational tracks that have long been the norm in parts of western Europe will likely not be adopted in nations like the United States, so the sorting into the workforce segments will be less efficient in the United States than in other nations. However, as data become more integrated from different sources, academic counselors will certainly adjust their methods in advising students – and their parents – into the best fitting secondary education programs.

We do not want to elide the discussion around the ethics such uses of data, as many societies have yet to really grapple with the ethical implications of "big data" and how it is used. One of the reasons why artificial intelligence and machine learning research lags in the European Union compared to China and United States is that the member nations of the European Union have more robustly debated the ethics around Big Data and those technologies. We believe that ethical and legal safeguards need to exist around Big Data and its uses. However, unless a global entity with real enforcement capabilities creates a worldwide ethical and legal framework around governance of these issues, it is likely that the types of data and their uses described above inevitably will occur. It is more likely that data security will take precedence over ethical concerns as we move forward in *the Fourth Industrial Revolution*. The cat, as they say, is out of the bag for better or worse. Likely both.

For human resources professionals, their long history of research and practice will position the field well to help employees across the workforce segments find success. What will challenge human resources professionals is that they will have to simultaneously operate, essentially, technologically augmented traditional human resources functions for employees while overseeing the strategic implementation and maintenance of intelligent applications and machines in the jobs that humans used to fill but are now filled by robots, algorithms, and intelligent machines. Consider this to be the equivalent of what Nobel Prize–winning economist Daniel Kahneman's best-selling book *Thinking, Fast and Slow*.

Kahneman summarized his and his colleague's work around the notion that humans have distinct modes of thinking: one based on emotion and instincts that operates quickly, and another based on logic and rational cognitive deliberation that operates slowly. The analog for future human resources professionals is the lightning quick processing of data and technologically driven human resources functions that algorithms and intelligent machines will take over: processing applicant data during selection, adjusting job descriptions and skill gaps, providing real-time performance management feedback through chatbots or personal performance management assistants, proactive recruitment through websites, tracking and filing safety and diversity and inclusion incidents and reports, and the like. On the other hand, human resources professionals will have to exhibit more deliberate judgment around strategic deployment of both human and machine resources. Moreover, human resources professionals more so than even now in the twenty-first century will have to understand the total business impact of these functions and strategic decisions across all segments of the workforce they oversee.

For example, in construction or health-care companies, human resources professionals will oversee employees responsible for technologies, devices, and neural networks of more singular artificial intelligence and smart machines. Human resources professionals will also oversee employees in business services or the medical professionals who treat patients or directly interact with customers. In construction companies, human resources professionals will also oversee skilled trades craftspeople who complete the core work of the business. In some health-care settings, such as hospitals, human resources professionals will also oversee skilled trades craftspeople that maintain facilities. Finally, in these example industries, human resources professionals will interface with government systems for government social safety net programs, as well as occupational health and safety programs. These professionals will also likely work with government agencies or outside staffing firms to place gig employees for short-term work assignments. All the while, human resources professionals of the future will work to maintain strategic integrity across human employees and work completed by machines. Thus, the future human resources professional will be not only an expert in traditional human resources for human employees but also technologists for the work done by machines. The ability to drive value across these different workforce segments and technological systems will require human resources professionals of the future to be complete businesspeople.

In the final chapter of this book, we will delve deeper into that gig employee segment of the workforce. However, we think it is important at this juncture to link some economic and compensation issues to educational issues that we previously discussed in this chapter. Earlier in the chapter, we described how educational systems will help sort citizens into the different workforce segments we described. This sorting will yield workforce segments of different sizes, with the highly technical segment of the workforce dedicated to developing, implementing, and maintaining the devices, machines, and networks of smart machines being the smallest of the workforce segments. Societies and businesses will fiercely compete in a global talent market for the highly skilled employees in this workforce segment. Thus, these employees will earn high levels of compensation. The employees in the business services segment of the workforce will also be comparatively smaller to the size of this workforce in 2020. Technological advances and smart machines will impact this workforce segment more than perhaps any other of the segments we have discussed. In the preface of this book, we explored the future of the accounting profession in the age of automation, artificial intelligence, and machine learning. Instead of deploying 10 auditors to a client, an accounting firm can deploy two data scientists and an auditor to the work that 10 auditors used to complete. This pattern will play out over and over between now and 2120. What this likely means from an economic perspective is that these types of professionals will see an imbalance of supply and demand whereby there will be more labor supply than demand. This will create fierce competition among employees in the labor market but will likely garner lower compensation levels than what we currently see in these types of professions.

Conversely, we will likely see robust supply and demand in the third segment of the workforce of the future that we described – skilled trades and high-end retail services. The value of human touch in these types of jobs will be in considerable demand. It is in these types of jobs and industries that we will see compensation levels vary across jobs and companies. Companies will look for competitive advantages in the human capital they acquire in these jobs, making this workforce segment analogous to what we currently see in jobs and industries around business services. Companies will compete for employees using varied compensation strategies. Some will lead the market, some will match the market, and some will lag the market. Some companies will differentiate based on skill-based compensation strategies. Others will emphasize total compensation packages to compete in the labor market. It is in the workforce segment that our current understanding of human resources practices will provide value to business operations but also be one of the more complex human resources environments. Deep labor markets, the use of technology to recruit and select, identifying human potential, providing immediate developmental performance feedback – technology aided or not, and robust training programs will be required to maximize the human and technological value to companies.

However, it is in the gig segment of the workforce, which will be large and varied, where human resources professionals might add the most value to future societies. Human resources knowledge and practice will greatly inform how societies cope with gig employees. The temporary nature of the work that any individual might do coupled with infinite individual differences and preferences for how humans can direct their energies and passions when not working will present the most complex challenge related to humans in the future of work and what that work means to societies. In the final chapter of this book, we will explore human creativity and the benefits that the gig workforce can provide to societies; but from a human resource management perspective, this segment of the workforce will require care.

Care is an important word and an important area of job growth in future societies. As we previously described a care worker, care workers will function in ways akin to what social workers or some government or nonprofit organization employees currently do. Yet the knowledge and skills required for those jobs will need to expand to include more direct knowledge of human resources. Vocational preferences, profile matching to companies or creative programs, knowledge of staffing functions for both gig work and creative programs, linking formal educational opportunities with lifelong learning opportunities, and managing robust human performance feedback systems will all be areas for care workers to gain expertise. Societies with large populations of technologically displaced citizens will need the care workers to maintain harmony – or close to it as possible – of populations where gaps between employed have's and have not's will be wide.

Finally, we return back to the need for educational opportunities that span any human's life. In Chapter 2 and Chapter 3, we discussed the importance of work to the human

psyche and its importance to societies. The role of education –
more specifically, learning – is central to the human condition.
Afterall, humans' ability to problem-solve and engage in
higher-order, abstract thinking separate our species from other
closely related species. From months-old children through
adults nearing the end of their lives, humans are driven to learn
and find meaning in learning. This drive will not subside in a
future more dominated by machines. Thus, societies will need
formal educational systems that span the human lifecycle.
Otherwise, to what ends or outlets will humans go to satisfy
their need to learn? Perhaps it is another possible paradox of
the *Fourth Industrial Revolution* that the more technology
societies deploy to remove humans from work, the more
cognitively engaged citizens will need to be.

Throughout this chapter, we have also hinted that these
types of societal changes will not occur uniformly across the
globe. Some nations currently utilize the advanced smart
technologies of the *Fourth Industrial Revolution* more than
others. In some cases, the utilization of these technologies is a
function of choice: some nations for ethical or legal reasons
limit the collection and use of data that underpin many of the
technologies we have discussed. In other cases, the differences
in the utilization of these technologies is a function of economic
development. In developing nations, citizens and businesses
alike might not possess the resources to develop, implement,
maintain, or adopt these technologies. Some nations might see
limited need for the use of these technologies based upon the
components of their overall economies. Over the next century,
the uneven adoption of the technologies associated with the
Fourth Industrial Revolution across the globe will present
challenges for human resources professionals, which we discuss
in the next chapter.

9

THE UNEVEN SPREAD OF THE FOURTH INDUSTRIAL REVOLUTION

The demise of human work might now be greatly overstated, depending upon where you live and work in the world. In previous chapters, we have described the increasingly accelerating wave of technology development, implementation, and adoption that will alter jobs, companies, industries, and economies. These changes will affect humans and societies in ways that in many circumstances contradict central parts of human identity and how societies have functioned for thousands of years. However, the societies that currently lead to development, implementation, and adoption of *Fourth Industrial Revolution* technologies have such a head start in these changes – and in fact have benefitted in many ways from other societies that have lagged in these changes – that the gaps between societies in the types of jobs lost, gained, or permanently displaced will always exist. That is, some societies will experience the waves of technological displacement that we have described in previous chapters with more frequency and depth than other societies. This is not to say that the effects of the *Fourth Industrial Revolution* will somehow skip or miss some nations while fundamentally altering other nations. Each nation will experience the effects of the *Fourth Industrial Revolution* but in different ways across different timelines.

To this point, we have mostly focused on how technology will continue to disrupt jobs, companies, industries, and economies of nations that have already seen high levels of technological penetration within such countries. The United States and China, in particular, have led the world not just in research and development but also in implementation of the technologies that will displace so many jobs and industries over the next 100 years.[1] The European Union, as a block of nations, ranks behind the United States and China, which suggest that even nations within the European Union vary on the intensity of technological advancement. Outside of these nations, India, Israel, South Korea, Singapore, and Australia have made large strides in developing, implementing, and adopting *Fourth Industrial Revolution* technologies.[2] Perhaps unsurprisingly, the least economically developed nations currently severely lag in the technological advancements that we see in advanced economies with Eastern Europe lagging Western Europe, Central Asia lagging Eastern Asia, most South American nations lagging Brazil, and most African nations lagging South Africa.[3]

We should not be surprised by the pattern of technological advancement across the globe, as economics likely explains the spread of the *Fourth Industrial Revolution* just like it has for previous industrial revolutions. Supply and demand of goods and services created the conditions for innovation, whether it was advances in farming to create excess supply to be exported to other nations or the development of technologies that made for easier production and consumption or exportation.[4] Wealthier nations could invest in technological advances – consider Enlightenment Europe's use of advancements in weapons and sailing technologies that allowed for resource exploitation of less advanced societies across the globe – to create new markets for new products and to produce more wealth. So, the cycle occurred over and over. Opportunity – or luck – also plays a role in these virtuous, self-reinforcing cycles, as Jared Diamond detailed in his Pulitzer Prize winning book *Guns, Germs, and Steel*. Sometimes ideal agricultural or animal herding climates provided one nation the necessary preconditions to economically develop at faster rates and gain permanent economic advantages than other not-as-fortunate nations.

Human resources professionals, while perhaps not thinking about these age-old dynamics, have quite a bit of understanding of differences between nations and economies from several perspectives. In many ways, the modern roots of human resources management as a strategic business partner began in the late 1970s. Until that point, human resources as a field had evolved as a combination of "personnel" functions and employee relations. The personnel function consisted of what we might now consider clerical or administrative functions – processing new hires, payroll and timecards, and organizing other benefits. Post World War II, the most developed economies featured strong manufacturing sectors as the backbone of those economies. This often meant high levels of union or organized labor activities. For instance, peak unionization rates of the US workforce occurred in the 1950s with the peak number of union-covered jobs occurring in the late 1970s.[5] Worldwide, unionization rates of workforces peaked in the mid-1980s.[6] During this post-war manufacturing and organized labor boom, human resources added labor and employee relations to functions covered in the field. Labor relations work directly related to managing the collective bargaining and contract implementation and maintenance processes. The employee relations aspect of human resources developed to acknowledge that employee well-being – that is, treating employees well – created positive work environments and reduced management–union conflict.

Simultaneously, advances in manufacturing – primarily coming from Japan's automotive manufacturing sector – began to displace the number of manufacturing employee required for those workforces. Higher wages and employee costs led manufacturers to not just implement technological advancements to the manufacturing production lines but also to search for supplies of lower cost labor. Therefore, the trend of offshoring or outsourcing jobs to foreign countries began. Vietnam became an early recipient of outsourced jobs, with apparel and shoe companies like Nike investing in manufacturing facilities and workforce development in that nation instead of in Nike's home in the United States. China has become a prime destination for manufacturing, especially electronics manufacturing. India has become an offshoring hotspot for information technology research and development, as well as call center support. Brazil has become a favored outsourcing destination for technology and manufacturing jobs. Eastern European nations like Poland and Bulgaria have become likely offshoring destinations for software development, technology services, and manufacturing. Russia, despite the challenges associated with corruption in that nation's private sector, benefits from its strong engineering educational system and has become an offshoring destination for engineering work.

The outsourcing or offshoring of jobs and the increased ease of conducting international trade, especially after the deconstruction of the former Soviet Bloc and the opening of China to Western businesses, have led human resources professionals to adapt to the challenges of operating multinational operations. A company with its corporate headquarters in one nation but with operational hubs in other nations will have to have human resources functions operating across national boundaries. A company's headquarters could send home nation employees abroad – expatriates – to help manage and develop the company's employees in a foreign location. Human resources professionals in the home country not only have to operate those functions in the home nation but also oversee those human resources functions in facilities overseas. While the basics of how human resources operate are the same across nations, important differences exist. Employment and labor laws, as well as national culture, affect the nature of employment contracts, working conditions, and the like. This means that human resources professionals in the home country must take into account the resulting effects of those laws and cultures on how they integrate their total human resources management systems. This presents challenges from a strategic human resources management perspective – linking functions horizontally and then vertically to the company's mission.

Looking at these effects on specific human resources functions is instructive. Take, for example, Siemens AG, the German-headquartered multinational technology, manufacturing, and business services company. Siemens operates office and facilities in every continent except Antarctica, in more than 60 countries. While European Union nations might share some common employment and labor laws, even differences across those nations exist in how employees are recruited, selected, compensation, trained, and managed. Occupational health and safety regulations across nations exist. Then apply that outside of continental Europe to North America or Asia. Coordinating the human resources practices across so many nations requires high levels of expertise and understanding. Does hiring employees in Germany differ from hiring employees in China? Does managing the performance of employees in the United States differ from managing the performance of employees in Vietnam? Of course, Siemens hires in-country human resources professionals to operate human resources functions and help link those to Siemens's overall mission; but the level of complexity of managing Siemens's total human capital is a massive undertaking.

From another perspective, current human resources professionals also understand and have expertise in international differences around the issue of global talent management. For many companies, recruiting and selection are international endeavors. Companies will search far and wide for high-skilled, in-demand employees. For higher level jobs within companies or jobs that possess unique skills, companies will recruit around the world. They will utilize proactive analytic tools to search for applicants on the Internet. They will engage international executive search firms to develop applicant pools. They will partner with institutions of higher education from around the world to identify talent. They will create complex company intranets to search for talent within their organizations and encourage current employees to apply for jobs. They will develop international managerial rotation programs that actually require employees to work outside of their home countries as expatriates for a specified period of time as a way to develop international talent that can move throughout the company regardless of where these employees call home.

Offshoring, outsourcing, and international staffing strategies have made current human resources professionals adept at understanding differences across nations; and another feature of current business has also allowed human resources professionals to think more strategically not only across a company's business but also across national boundaries. Prior to the so-called *Knowledge Economy* that emerged from the manufacturing-based economies of the late 1970s and early 1980s, most companies operated their supply chains within much smaller geographic regions. It was not uncommon for a company based in a home country to have all its suppliers also be located in the same country. Again, as trade barriers and political and economic unions such as the European Union and the Soviet Bloc rose and fell, not only did the movement of labor change but so too did the movement of suppliers. As global supply chains have become more integrated and interconnected, it is common for dominant companies within a supply chain to exert managerial influence over smaller companies in a supply chain. This happens not just with inventory management, transportation practices, or manufacturing systems but also with human resources practices. This means that human resources best practices can be transmitted through large portions of the total supply chain. It also means that human resources professionals in companies will integrate human resources practices across the supply chain. After all, if a vital company in a supply chain experiences high employee turnover, that will affect the performance of the supply chain in total.

Taken together, current human resources professionals have become true business partners within companies. These professionals have learned lessons from other business functions within companies and applied these practices to human resources functions. This includes adapting to the variance of businesses across international boundaries and cultures. The knowledge gained over the past decades has prepared human resources professionals to adapt to the variance of adoption of smart technologies across national barriers and cultures.

Perhaps understanding how global supply chains have spread provides an analogous paradigm to understand how the adoption of automation, artificial intelligence, and machine learning will unevenly spread across the planet and create challenges for human resources professionals of the future. Also, recall from Chapter 3 that decision-making around the development, implementation, and adoption of those technologies will come down to cost-benefit analyses by most companies. The cost of developing robots, for example, can be prohibitive. Companies and universities regularly develop these types of technologies without plans to actually implement them into a business. Sometimes, they seek to develop technologies as a way to understand important concepts or related activities around the technology. If the costs of developing a robot remain too cost prohibitive – that is, the robot costs more than hiring human employees – companies will not deploy the robot. However, as the cost of developing and implementing the robot decreases, business decision-makers will explore the long-term value of implementing the robot to replace human employees.

What we have seen over the last three to four decades is that companies will not deploy robots or other forms of automation as a first line of decision-making. Companies will seek to outsource or offshore facets of work to other businesses that can produce the work at a lower cost than the company can produce itself. Maybe that supporting business in the supply chain operates in the same country as the company. Maybe that supporting business in the supply chain operates in a different country. Wherever the supporting business operates, the company will decide to outsource or offshore based upon cost without sacrificing quality. Consider the example of the toy and entertainment company, Hasbro.

Hasbro originated in the United States near Providence in the state of Rhode Island, just south of Massachusetts and about an hour's drive from Boston. Over the past three or four decades, Hasbro has closed many manufacturing plants in the United States and offshored the manufacturing of its toy and gaming products mainly to China. Hasbro has invested hundreds of millions of dollars – if not billions – over this period of time to build out facilities in China and secure its supply chains for products and distribution to markets. At the start of this process, the total costs of establishing a global supply chain and manufacturing base in China were less than doing this work in the United States. However, over the same period of time as countless companies have repeated the same process and offshored manufacturing to China, changes in the Chinese labor market have begun to alter the cost-benefit business analysis of the entire model. First, China's "one child" policy and the nation's simultaneous economic growth have created lower birth rates of children.[7] In fact, by the next century, China's population will dramatically decrease as India's and Nigeria's populations will exceed China's. Second, as the demand for workers boomed in Chinese cities and regions to where many Western companies offshored their work, rural Chinese citizens flocked to these destinations to find work – with the side effect of leaving millions of parentless children back in their villages and towns.[8] The combined effects of these factors are that China has experienced a lower supply of workers as demand for their work has increased. Moreover, after decades of developing a class of professional Chinese managers through higher education and the mentoring of Western business expatriates, China has experienced the growth of a large and vibrant professional class of employees. Simply put, labor costs more in China now than it did three or four decades ago. When you add in the costs of shipping finished products from China back around the world – commodity prices for oil and other fuels add variable expenses, as does now securing container ships and commercial shipping lanes from open-water pirates – companies must now make new calculations about the cost-benefit of setting up permanent manufacturing in China.

For a company like Hasbro, what might this mean? Will they continue to invest in its Chinese facilities, distribution, and transportation systems? Will Hasbro explore other offshore locations where the cost of business is cheaper? Vietnam possesses the transportation infrastructure – roads, ports – and an already developed managerial class to operate Western supply chain activities. India similarly has well-developed workforces and infrastructure to support work that Hasbro might complete. Bangladesh has emerged as an offshoring garment manufacturing hotspot but does not have the depth of workforce development as China, Vietnam, and India. Does Hasbro look to Eastern Europe to move its manufacturing operations? Or does it look to Brazil and its growing hub of offshored work? Hasbro might also consider reshoring work back to the United States, as Apple did in the late 2010s in support of some of their product lines.

The technological implications for these decisions are great. Hasbro could maintain its well-established manufacturing and supply chain hubs in China but, given the rising costs of labor in China, decide to invest in more automation and smart intelligence to conduct work instead of human employees. What about the impact of chatbots or virtual assistants on the highly developed Indian workforce? Many United States and Great British companies offshored call centers to India over the past three decades. Do these artificially intelligent chatbots and virtual assistants now displace the call center employees in Delhi, Hyderabad, and Bangalore? As the accounting profession in Western nations begins its gradual contraction due to outsourcing to India and Russia, as well as through algorithms and data analysts, do those same algorithms reduce the need for offshored work in those foreign nations? Will Western hospitals still require overseas X-ray and other diagnostic work to be completed overnight by employees halfway around the world when algorithms and smart machines will complete the work in a faction of the time – perhaps within minutes of a scan or test – than a human employee is capable of regardless of where that human might live?

Rebalancing the offshored and outsourced work across the globe will create the same types of challenges that we have discussed with the displacement of jobs within countries that will more intensely adopt the technologies of the *Fourth Industrial Revolution*. Earlier in this chapter, we listed the United States, China, and the European Union as the top three locations for the development, implementation, and adoption of automation, artificial intelligence, and machine learning technologies. This should not surprise anyone given that those areas represent the largest economies in the world; however, if we were to project which nations will likely move ahead in similar technological advancements over the next century, we should again look to nations that currently rank highly as destination nations for outsourcing and offshoring jobs. The rationale is fairly straightforward. The nations investing in advanced technologies also represent some of the largest importers or beneficiaries of jobs from an outsourcing and offshoring perspective. As, for example, companies in the European Union – where the Ireland, Spain, Germany, and France rank highly among European Union member nations in smart technology advancements – outsource or offshore jobs to lower labor cost nations, technology from those Western European nations will follow into the offshore nations. From a global supply chain perspective, dominant companies in a supply chain will similarly push its technology through the supply chain. This currently happens with knowledge transfer of best practices; it will likely occur with the transfer of technology to less wealthy nations.

One-hundred years from now, we should expect to see currently developing economies in nations such as Indonesia, Brazil, Vietnam, Philippines, Thailand, and Chile adopt and implement more smart technology. Why these nations? These nations currently rank highly in destination countries for offshoring and outsourcing jobs.[9] This will present challenges, however, for these destination nations, as well as already established offshoring behemoths like China and India. As the automation of manufacturing processes spreads to these less economically developed nations and as artificial intelligence and machine learning technologies like chatbots reduce the need for call center–type work, four jobs will be eliminated for every one new job created.

Throughout this book, we have hypothesized that the velocity in which jobs will be displaced by the technologies of the *Fourth Industrial Revolution* will create disruption to individuals, companies, industries, and societies. We have described these displacements as occurring in cycles whereby technology moves quicker to displace jobs than to create new jobs. Wealthier societies possess the resources to deal with these disruptive cycles more easily than less wealthy societies. Now consider that many of the nations that have benefitted from offshoring and outsourcing of jobs from wealthier nations will then be exposed to the same disruptive forces of technology that will roil those wealthy nations over the next 100 years. The key question here – one to which we have no answer – is, can the currently developing economies mature fast enough to deal with the technological disruptions to their societies in ways that wealthier nations do? Given the long lens of history around persistent wealth gaps between nations, we worry that by the time the *Fourth Industrial Revolution* comes for the less advanced economies of the world, the persistent inequalities between advanced and developing economies will widen.

We again do not want to elide a discussion of the ethics around technologies associated with the *Fourth Industrial Revolution*. However, we believe that the implications of the spread of technologies from wealthier to less wealthy nations need to be discussed in greater detail, especially from an ethical perspective. European Union member nations currently debate the ethical implications for advanced technologies and big data more vigorously than does the United States or

China. We already know that a technology gap exists between wealthy and less wealthy citizens. We previously outlined possible workforces of the future that break down along the lines of who will have full-time employment and who will gig for employment opportunities. It is also hard to have current ethical debates about future events that may or may not occur. Yet, we do believe that more thought needs to be given to what it means to have a world where highly wealthy and technologically advanced nations first outsource or offshore hundreds of millions of jobs to less wealthy and technologically advanced nations only to then have technology eliminate the very jobs that were outsourced or offshored.

For human resources professionals that work for organizations that do outsource and offshore work to foreign nations – as well as likely spread technological advancements to those nations – the speed of technological penetration to those destination nations will vary from country to country. Again, using supply chain framing, dominant companies will push technology down through its supply chain, which could take decades. Managing the human capital associated with the type of globalized work activity will require high-level strategic thinking and integration with the technology functions within companies. Human resources professionals working in multinational companies must involve themselves in the business discussion about decisions to implement technologies that will displace jobs not just in the company headquarters but also across the multinational enterprise.

We again turn to the notion of thinking fast and slow as we previously applied to human resources professionals in Chapter 5. The spread of technologies associated with the *Fourth Industrial Revolution* will not occur quickly or evenly across the globe, even within a multinational company. National cultures and legal structures will either accelerate or decelerate the adoption of smart technologies. This means from an enterprise human resources perspective, human resources professionals will work in environments that will contain both smart technologies and legacy human resources systems. On the one hand, all of the smart technologies we have discussed in this book applied to human resources management will greatly increase the speed in which human resources functions operate. On the other hand, international human resources professionals will operate human resources functions in other nations that move at the speed of humans and not machines. Of course, algorithms and smart machines will assist human resources professionals in managing a company's or organization's human capital regardless of where that human capital is located; however, the human employees they work with across nations will require a human touch. Again, as we have previously espoused, the more that technology infuses human environments, the more value that human-to-human contact carries.

As we begin our transition into the final chapter of this book, we pause to consider the societal implications for the international spread and proliferation of smart technologies. It is possible, perhaps even likely, that some societies will develop in response to the *Fourth Industrial Revolution* by reorganizing workforces that map onto the technological advances. Yet other societies will evolve at slower paces to these technological advances. You might think "this is not different than we see today with wealthy and less wealthy societies," and that might be the case. After all, we have seen persistent wealth gaps between nations for centuries. Yet it seems to us, as we have consistently said throughout this book, that the *Fourth Industrial Revolution* feels different than previous industrial revolutions. How much conflict – both within societies and between societies – will develop as the *Fourth Industrial Revolution* unevenly spreads across the globe, completely reshaping some societies while perhaps leaving other societies completely behind? Even recent human history suggests that conflict will occur within and between nations as technology and the wealth it generates ripples across the globe. We do not expect a *Terminator*-style future where machines and human fight for domination; rather we suspect that human conflict over technological advances will occur.

Within societies, however, a world of machines doing most of the work of societies might usher in an era unprecedented human well-being. Such is the focus of the final chapter of this book. What would humans do if they did not have to work, and how could societies still thrive without human work?

10

A TECHNOLOGY-ENABLED FUTURE RENAISSANCE?

Algorithms, virtual chatbots, connected smart devices, neural networks, smart machines, and, compared to today, fewer humans working in technologically advanced economies is one possible, if not likely, future. This future might alarm some, as technology cannot unwind and replace millions of years of evolution for modern humans and the societies built by those humans. Our human drive to work, to direct our energies and motivation into productive outcomes, and to identify with what we do as work will not disappear even amid the rapid acceleration of technology that will potentially deprive us of a core dimension of our species. Humans, in response to the unrelenting incursion of technology into our lives, will do what we have always done: let's work the problem, people! Except now the problem we must solve is a most difficult one: what do we do with fewer work opportunities and what are the implications of this for societies? It need not all be bleak and dystopic outcomes we have seen in the movies.

Even within technologically advanced societies that will see smaller workforces, humans will still work. As we have previously detailed, the very data companies and governments collect now through our social media engagement, our shopping and Internet search histories, our educational and extracurricular activities, our medical and well-being histories, and our interests will create connections between us now and our offspring. Algorithms will predict educational opportunities and human development opportunities for just born infants. Technology will remove easy-to-do and highly repetitive activities from our daily lives, freeing us to pursue other value-added activities in our lives. Care workers – armed with a century or more of human resources, social work, mental health, and well-being processes, practices, and techniques – will help us to live better lives.

The fundamental paradox we have previously described will remain: as technology takes over more and more of our lives, we will value human interaction more and more. The value-added human interaction will be seen in the education systems in these technologically advanced societies. Future young learners will not have robots or hologram chatbots replace human teachers, even if teachers will deploy those technologies in their classrooms to maximize student learning potential. Human interaction will remain vital in technologically advanced societies, as it will always be humans who will teach us how to be human and nurture our humanity. Perhaps this means that as students learn about more advanced technologies at younger ages, subjects such as philosophy, art, and music will also be introduced at early ages in a student's learning environment. Despite smart machines having the ability to create beautiful music, art, or poetry for our enjoyment over the next century, creating those forms of art will reinforce our understanding of our humanness.

However, these early and ongoing educational opportunities will feed into the systems that will sort humans into the different workforces that we described in Chapter 8. Students' knowledge, skills, abilities, successes, failures, and interests will leave a long data trail that will help universities, employers, and governments identify opportunities to maximize each person's potential. In some ways, we will see choice removed from our lives. Some might argue that all of these data are not completely determinative of our futures, that human choice will always create unpredictability. In other ways, however, the systems and infrastructure that will guide forthcoming generations into their personal futures will provide more choice. The long trails of data that we will leave from birth onward will enable care workers to develop profiles – of educational opportunities, of career opportunities, of interest opportunities, of sporting opportunities, of art opportunities – into which individuals might fit. As a forty-year-old adult right now, you might stumble through your life not knowing that you possibly possessed the requisite skills or potential to find success in another work discipline or even sporting activity. Imagine a future where you have multiple pathways identified earlier in life, where your potential opportunities – not singular but multiple – are known to you at a much earlier time in your life and you can choose which paths – again, not singular but multiple – you can walk. Perhaps you can find more fulfilment in your life if you have a better understanding of who you are and what you are capable of at an earlier age.

Similarly, college or university will provide formative experiences for humans. While the workforces we mentioned in Chapter 8 will still require employees, the supply of labor will outpace the demand of employers or industries in most technologically advanced societies. Yet those employers and industries will continue to need deep pools of highly skilled and trained employees to choose from as they fill vacant positions. However, from a healthy society perspective, education in and of itself provides significant benefits to citizens and societies. We need not quote Socrates here. In the early twenty-first century, some began to debate the value of humanities and arts majors at colleges and universities. After all, why would a student, parent, or government want to potentially spend hundreds of thousands of dollars for an undergraduate degree in philosophy when that degree holder can only find a job that pays significantly less per year than jobs available to other less rigorous majors? Or so this thinking goes, as if starting salary is the only measure of worth of a person or their value to a society. In a future where technology reduces employment opportunities for so many citizens of many nations, the failure to better educate citizens will lead to the dystopic visions that Hollywood writers imagined in *The Matrix*, *Total Recall*, and the *Terminator* franchises. Perhaps just as frightening, uneducated citizens will lead slothful or dull-witted populations and societies that have lost their inabilities to critically think – the very topic of the dark comedy Mike Judge film *Idiocracy*. It is that world that Orwell, Huxley, Fuller, or Bradbury might have feared most.

Much like any point in time but more so during industrial revolutions, challenges will exist creating, developing, and maintaining these technologically advanced societies. We have previously discussed inequalities emerging within societies related to work and the resources accrued through that work but also between societies that have gaps between technological advancements and the societal wealth accrued through those advances. Within societies where work opportunities are not equally distributed, rigid class systems can form. After all, if a hundred years' worth of familial data can shape opportunities for a future generation, that future generation can be essentially locked into work, educational, or economic strata without any individual merit. Conversely, individuals can be locked out of opportunities because of their ancestors' long data trail that might exclude them from opportunities. Data always contain some amount of error, and variance around data always present problems for those who make decisions. This again reinforces the need for robust educational opportunities and multiple potential paths for future generations to choose. Data will not make the decisions; humans will need to use data to make decisions.

The possible workforces of the future that we detailed in Chapter 5 also can create inequalities between those workforces and hence within societies. Employees tending to the neural networks of smart machines will likely command higher levels of compensation and benefit from the resources they earn through their work. Employees working to support core business services – even medical and legal professionals – will face fierce labor market competition and disruption from an oversupply of qualified applicants, which can depress the compensation for those employees. Employees working in the skilled or construction trades or high-end retail industries will command higher levels of compensation because of the value of human touch required to perform these jobs. Then we suspect a large gig workforce will emerge in the future of technologically advanced societies. Gig employees will have intermittent work opportunities and thus intermittent financial earning opportunities. It is not that gig employees will not possess high levels of motivation or in-demand skills and abilities. They will. It is that the industries and jobs in which these employees might have worked in the past will no longer exist. What will societies do with these citizens – educated, motivated, skilled, but lacking opportunities?

The scope of human history suggests that inequality – financial, educational, opportunities – results in negative societal outcomes. The harsh economic sanctions placed on Germany due to their participation in World War I created anxiety and unrest among citizens of the nation, which led to the emergence of national socialism and a second world war. Unemployed former soldiers in the United States who were promised pensions for their service during World War I camped out on the banks of the Anacostia River in Washington, DC, amid the Great Depression, threatening to march on the Capitol unless the government fulfilled its promises led to the fundamental changes that Franklin Roosevelt's New Deal delivered. Over and over throughout history, leaving large segments of any population economically behind or opportunity deprived leads to civilian unrest or even revolutions. This is all evidenced by the events of the summer of 2020 in which many Americans protested the unequal promises of equal opportunity.

Governments will often broaden social safety nets to attempt to limit these types of inequalities. We predict that the governments of the technologically advanced societies of the *Fourth Industrial Revolution* will not just strengthen educational and human development opportunities for their citizens; they will more robustly engage policies that directly compensate citizens not for the work that they perform but for their citizenship. We refer here to what are known as *universal basic income* programs. Universal basic income – often known by its acronym of UBI – has existed in many forms across nations. Some might consider unemployment benefits as a form of UBI, although unemployment benefits are often tied to job search and often expire over specified periods of time. Some might also consider government-sponsored or backed retirement systems as forms of UBI. Many western societies have these types of government-backed retirement systems or pensions. Citizens work for specified periods of time, dutifully paying into the system through their tax contributions, and receive retirement benefits for the remainder of their lives. In the United States, Social Security acts as baseline retirement benefit system. Canada's Pension Plan and Old Age Security act in a similar fashion. The United Kingdom operates mandatory participation state pensions. Australia operates a multitiered national pension system. Scandinavian nations – Norway, Sweden, Finland, Iceland, and Demark – are known for their generous first-class national pension systems.

Yet the UBI programs that we suspect will proliferate across the most technologically advanced societies of the future will operate more like the State of Alaska's *Alaska Permanent Fund*. Enacted through state-level legislative procedures in 1978, the Alaska Permanent Fund pays yearly dividends – of roughly $1,600 – to all eligible citizens of the state. Eligibility for the yearly dividend consists of establishing permanent residency in Alaska for a calendar year beginning on January 1 of the year. Taxes generated from oil exploration, levied by the state on for-profit companies, fund the Permanent Fund. As of the year 2020, the Alaska Permanent Fund has over $65 billion of assets under management. Alaskans value the fund so dearly that in 2019 – prior to the economic recession triggered by the COVID-19 pandemic – that Alaska's governor slashed $130 million from the state's flagship higher education system, which forced the shuttering of campuses and programs, rather than tap into the Alaska Permanent Fund for temporary relief[1].

While Alaska's Permanent Fund represents perhaps the longest running UBI program in the world, other jurisdictions and nations have long experimented with different forms of UBI. Nations across the globe have experimented with various forms of UBI to address myriad issues. Iran implemented a modest national income designed to help its working poor purchase goods such as gasoline. In 2015, Finland launched a three-year experimental UBI program to understand and better determine if the program could scale nationwide. In the Canadian province of Manitoba in the mid-1970s, the town of Dauphin was the site of a UBI experiment where lower-income residents of the town received direct cash payments to supplement their working wages. In Kenya, more than 20,000 citizens across hundreds of small villages have received a modest – less than one US dollar – daily payment over the past 12 years. Nearly 6,000 Indian citizens in the state of Madhya Pradesh received direct monthly universal income payments for a year. In the United States city of Stockton, California, which regularly is rated among the most difficult cities in which to live in the United States, over 100 citizens have received $500 per month over an eighteen-month period beginning in 2018. Studies of these UBI programs repeatedly find evidence that such programs increase educational, nutritional, physical and mental health, and overall well-being outcomes[2].

However, despite the nearly universally positive outcomes associated with these pilot programs, questions persist about the programs. Depending upon one's political beliefs, you might assume – and have even repeatedly heard – that simply giving people money that directly is not tied to work or job searching outcomes will result in people dropping out of the labor force. Why would someone want to work if they already receive government-funded income? Perhaps one might also have heard that such cash transfers will result in unhealthy consumer spending behaviors – illegal drugs, gambling, lotteries, alcohol, cigarettes, and the like. Since people do not "work" for this money, will they not throw it away on frivolous purchases that they would not do with their own money? From a national budgetary perspective, perhaps one might wonder about the fiscal sustainability of paying citizens UBI. How do you pay for UBI without overtaxing your population? As with the positive outcomes found for citizens receiving forms of UBI, research on these programs finds little to no evidence of the feared negative outcomes espoused by critics of UBI. In fact, it appears that citizens receiving these funds use the monies to pay for basic living needs – food, rent, medical care, and the like. Importantly, the same research suggests little to no effect on labor participation rates. It seems that people, as we outlined in Chapter 1, find work an important part of their identity and will continue to work while having their wages supplemented by UBI funds. To further support this, during the COVID-19 pandemic, many United States citizens received $600 per month of additional unemployment benefits beyond what is typically received; and the Chicago Federal Reserve reported that citizens receiving these additional monies were actually more dedicated to finding a new job. Once those benefits expired, those citizens' job search intensity disappeared[3]. That is, people worked harder to find work when receiving unemployment benefits than they do when they do not receive those benefits.

The economic impact of these programs is important to consider, especially as we fully enter the *Fourth Industrial Revolution* and begin to experience the cyclical shocks of technology-abetted job displacement. For those who followed the 2020 United States presidential campaign and election, a candidate for the Democratic Party nomination, Andrew Yang, openly advocated for a $1,000 per month "Freedom Dividend" that every American should receive in response to the technological displacement of jobs and industries across the nation. Yang feared that the *Fourth Industrial Revolution* would create mass economic and social anxiety that would result in havoc in cities and states across the nation. Companies would still accrue wealth and the economy would continue to expand as smart machines slowly and inexorably take over work formerly completed by human employees, but the citizens displaced by the wave of technology would be left behind. Yang proposed a 10% value-added tax on businesses to fund the Freedom Dividend for every citizen over the age of 18[4]. Yang, of course, is not the only politician or member of a political party advocating for the adoption of robust UBI programs, with political parties in Germany, France, Switzerland, Ireland, Australia, and other nations arguing for such nationwide programs.

What Yang and many others argue is that as technology displaces jobs at greater rates than any new jobs created, aggregate demand for products, goods, and services will decline. Simply, if people do not have money, they cannot purchase goods. In large economies based on consumer spending, having a large percentage of your population unable to earn livable earnings will obviously lead to a deep recession. In fact, in the 2008 Great Recession, the lack of aggregate demand lengthened and deepened that recession[5]. Citizens' lack of disposable income led to a reinforcing cycle of business closures, employee layoffs, and less consumer spending. From this perspective, implementing universal income programs in the face of impending and likely permanent reductions in the size of workforces across economically and technologically advanced nations seems like a beneficial strategy to maintain an economy's aggregate demand while also directly helping those citizens in most need of financial assistance.

We do not envision a future of large segments of any nation's population simply no longer working. As we previously suggested, it is likely that a large and robust gig workforce will exist. Societies will still require robust educational and human development opportunities and systems. Millions of years of human evolution will simply not unwind over the next century. People will still find meaning in work; however, the nature of work for many citizens will fundamentally change. The idea of a full-time, thirty-to-forty-hour work week job will not be available to many even though they will possess the requisite skills and motivation to possess those jobs. People will still want to own homes, start families, raise children, purchase goods and services, and live meaningful and fulfilling lives. Economies will still function on the creation of wealth through the production of products, goods, and services purchased by people, businesses, and governments. Work will still be vital to humans. Yet what do we do with gig workforces that vary in work opportunities and wages?

As we previously mentioned in this chapter and in Chapter 8, new care positions that combined the knowledge of many fields – human resources prominently among those fields – will operate at the intersection of government programs, employment opportunities, and job search for gig workforce members. Data and algorithms, of course, will facilitate the identification of employment opportunities and gig job seekers. Gig workforce employees will likely transition between the other, full-time employment workforces, as opportunities become available and fit between the job, company, and gig employee are achieved. Conversely, members of those full-time employment workforces will also transition into and out of the gig workforce depending on multiple factors such as employee performance, company performance, economic recessions, and continued technological advancements that will displace employees. Mostly, we think it's likely that gig employees will have opportunities that we might now recognize as part-time or contract work. Perhaps these care positions dedicated to employment will function similarly to how temporary employment or staffing companies operate currently but at broader, more integrated levels than these types of firms operate today.

The interface with government agencies will remain a vital piece of the care workers dedicated to the gig workforce of the future. Differences between the workforces of the future in terms of compensation, opportunities, and the movement between the workforces likely mean that any UBI programs will require means testing. Means testing refers to the determination of how much of any service or program that any individual will qualify to receive. In the case of UBI, a means-tested income benefit would help offset the amount of income a gig employee would require compared to the amount a professional services employee would receive. You might ask yourself, "Why would a fulltime employee receive universal basic income at all?" Simply, for equity – or fairness – reasons. Every member of a society that has a UBI should qualify for some level of the benefit, as nations will need buy-in from all of its citizens to maintain these programs. What will be important is for means testing to reduce income and wealth gaps to healthier levels, as higher levels of income and wealth inequality are often associated with negative individual and societal outcomes[6]. Thus, for gig employees who have lower levels of base income due to the briefer nature of their work engagements, governments should deliver higher levels of basic income to citizens in that workforce compared to citizens in other workforces that earn higher wages. This is not to say that all citizens will earn the same amount of combined income. They will not, but gig employees will need to obtain livable wages to allow them to participate in the benefits of progress.

There are also national implications for the administration of UBI programs. In large population countries like the United States, China, and India, the implementation of UBI programs will serve different purposes than smaller population countries like the Netherlands, Norway, and Denmark, for example. Job and industry displacement due to the technologies of the *Fourth Industrial Revolution* will disproportionately influence smaller population nations. Denmark has a population of just under six million people, of which three million are in

Denmark's workforce. Nearly 80% of Denmark's economy is tied to private employers, and only 2% of its population works in agricultural industries. Denmark's workforce is highly concentrated in services – financial, business, technology – and has a small manufacturing base[7]. This is exactly the profile of an economy that will see significant labor force disruption as smart machine technology matures and displaces employees. For a nation like Denmark, what happens when more than half of your population has its work at risk of displacement from technology? Will young, educated Danes leave Denmark to pursue job opportunities abroad? Will Denmark be left with an aging, retired population as most of its working-age population must leave in order to pursue working opportunities elsewhere? Or will Denmark implement a robust universal income program to keep Danes from leaving their country? This type of problem for smaller, wealthy, technologically advanced nations is very different than the problems that the United States will have as technological advancements roil its society. For the United States, social cohesion will be a huge problem; for Denmark, its very nationhood could be at stake.

For all nations affected by the *Fourth Industrial Revolution*, figuring out what to do with idle citizens' hands could be a concern. If UBI provides economic stability for its citizens while also maintaining aggregate economic demand – purchasing of products, goods, and service – and smart technologies continue to add wealth to businesses and nations through taxation of those business, what do nations do with gig employees who cannot work full-time? Let us ask you: what would you do with your time if you did not have to worry about work? Would you put your interests into action? Would you take your creativity and apply it to the world around you? We believe it is highly unlikely that you will simply sit in your home and idle for days, weeks, and months.

The quick COVID-related shutdown of 2020 left many without much to do, but eventually most settled into positive life patterns. We suspect that you will direct your energies into things about which you are passionate.

You might not think of yourself as creative, as we typically think about creativity as solely residing in the domains of art, marketing, or new product design. Creativity refers to the development of novel ideas. Creativity requires imagination. Creativity requires original thought. It does not require a palette and canvas. It does not require knowledge of music theory or musical instrument mastery. It does not require mastery of a language, character development, and story development or composition skills. After all, when Argentinian footballer, Lionel Messi, dribbles a ball and whirls through an opponent's defensive players, is he not creative? Does he not conjure movements out of his imagination and implement those on the field? Or perhaps you like to garden and imagine what your ideal garden looks like. What types of seeds would you plant? Where would you plant them? How would you care for them? What would you do with your harvest?

Harvard Business School professor Teresa Amabile has theorized that our affect – how we feel at any given time – represents a crucial feature of creativity[8]. When people have a positive state of mind, they are more likely to have creative thoughts. If people remain in this positive state of mind and can think through the implications of their creative thoughts, it is much more likely that these creative thoughts can lead to action. That is, creativity can move from thinking to action – or innovation. Innovation requires creative thoughts that can be implemented. The difference between creativity and innovation comes down to whether or not the creative thoughts are useful and thus implementable. This view of creativity includes not just traditional outlets for creativity like the arts but also of problem-solving. In Chapter 4 of this book, we described a fundamental feature of humans. That of problem-solving. Humans continually seek to improve efficiency. Humans continually seek to remove barriers. Humans continually seek to make our lives and societies better. In fact, it is this very drive that has led to the development, implementation, and adoption of the technologies of the *Fourth Industrial Revolution* that will likely limit if not completely remove for some people the opportunities to work.

One hundred years from now with smart technology providing humans more time to think less about work and with governments likely removing pressure to earn livable wages by providing UBI, many people in societies around the globe will have the freedom to pursue their passions. They can direct the energies they would have otherwise devoted to work into improving other facets of their lives or societies. Our long data trails will help care workers to identify nonwork opportunities into which we can invest our energies. Our personal smart technologies will assist us in our planning and execution of creative thoughts we have as we seek to convert our thoughts into action. In short, we think it is possible that the unprecedented adoption and usage of technology, while potentially destroying work opportunities, will create the environment for a second Renaissance to emerge. As humans seek to connect with each other and to connect with the aspects of our lives that make us human, an explosion of creativity will occur that benefits societies. In another paradox of the *Fourth Industrial Revolution*, technology will free humans to create a more pleasant and beautiful world.

For human resource management professionals, the future will become more complex than our current world. Human resources professionals will have more than a century of know-how in the operation of strategic human resources systems. They will be able to think fast and slow so as to maintain legacy human resources functions in areas of industry or areas of the world that will not have adopted or as heavily adopted the technologies of the *Fourth Industrial Revolution* while also be able to use those technologies when needed. The "people" employees to which human resources professionals are often referred will, like most business professionals of the future, also be technologists. Moreover, the field of human resources will continue to expand and integrate into other "people" focused fields like social work, counseling, and other human service professions. Our knowledge of how to recruit, select, compensate, manage, and train people will need to expand to help manage opportunities for those in and out of the gig workforce. Like a cruise ship coordinator, human resources professionals will help identify nonwork opportunities and pathways for people; and this will likely mean that many of our skills will be applied to educational systems. Moving students through more fine-tuned academic programs – university or technical tracks that begin during secondary educational systems – will require the exact know-how that human resources professionals have long since developed and mastered. In short, while so many jobs will go away, human resources professionals will continue to add value to a world of fewer employees.

Throughout the pages of this book, we have focused on a future that might create quite a bit of consternation or anxiety among all of us. We have not grappled with whether or not societies *should* implement and adopt automation, artificial intelligence, and machine learning. In our minds, the genie has left the bottle and the toothpaste is out of the tube! What we have detailed in this book is why we think work will remain important to humans and societies and what might happen as work becomes less important for large swaths of human populations. In particular, we have focused on the role that our field of human resources management will play in what

we think is the inexorable march to a more automated, connected, and smart technological world. We feel confident that
human resources will expand its role from the workplace to
helping societies. Some might disagree with our views, and we
think that disagreements are important as we plan for a future
that we know will contain smart machines. As Calvin said in
his last words to comic friend and antagonist Hobbes – it's a
magical world, Hobbes, ol' buddy – let's go exploring.
Consider your imagination provoked!

NOTES

PREFACE

1. Accountants & Auditors. (n.d.). Retrieved from https://datausa.io/profile/soc/accountants-auditors. Accessed on January 14, 2020.
2. Sheedy, C. (2017, June 26). *What CPAs need to do to survive the automation revolution.* Retrieved from https://www.journalofaccountancy.com/newsletters/2017/jun/survive-automation-revolution.html. Accessed on January 14, 2020.
3. Cohn, M., Stimpson, J., & Pozo, I. (2013, July 10). *Companies plan to expand accounting outsourcing.* Retrieved from https://www.accountingtoday.com/news/companies-plan-to-expand-accounting-outsourcing. Accessed on January 21, 2020.
4. Vincent, J. (2017, November 30). *Automation threatens 800 million jobs, but technology could still save us, says report.* Retrieved from https://www.theverge.com/2017/11/30/16719092/automation-robots-jobs-global-800-million-forecast. Accessed on January 16, 2020.

CHAPTER 1

1. Zaleskiewicz, T., Gasiorowska, A., & Vohs, K. D. (2017, June 23). *The psychological meaning of money.* Retrieved from https://onlinelibrary.wiley.com/doi/abs/10.1002/9781118926352.ch7. Accessed on January 22, 2020.
2. Donkin, R. (2010). *The history of work.* Basingstoke: Palgrave Macmillan.

3. Groeneveld, E. (2021, January 11). *Prehistoric hunter-gatherer societies*. Retrieved from https://www.ancient.eu/article/991/prehistoric-hunter-gatherer-societies/. Accessed on January 19, 2020.

4. Weir, K. (2013, December). *More than job satisfaction*. Retrieved from https://www.apa.org/monitor/2013/12/job-satisfaction. Accessed on January 23, 2020.

5. Amabile, T. M., Barsade, S. G., Mueller, J. S., & Staw, B. M. (2005). Affect and creativity at work. *Administrative Science Quarterly, 50*(3), 367–403.

6. Dave, D., Rashad, I., & Spasojevic, J. (2006, March 27). *The effects of retirement on physical and mental health outcomes*. Retrieved from https://www.nber.org/papers/w12123. Accessed on January 23, 2020.

7. Vandenbrouke, G. (2020, February 26). *How many people will be retiring in the years to come?*. Retrieved from https://www.stlouisfed.org/on-the-economy/2019/may/how-many-people-will-be-retiring-in-the-years-to-come. Accessed on January 24, 2020.

CHAPTER 2

1. Grand Valley State University. (n.d.). Retrieved from https://www.gvsu.edu/fobi/family-firm-facts-5.htm. Accessed on February 14, 2020.

2. Reuss, A. (2011, March 31). *What's behind union decline in the United States?*. Retrieved from http://www.dollarsandsense.org/archives/2011/0311reuss2.html. Accessed on February 2, 2020.

3. Union Members Summary. (2020, January 22). Retrieved from https://www.bls.gov/news.release/union2.nr0.htm

4. McCarthy, N. (2017, June 20). *Which countries have the highest levels of labor union membership?* [Infographic]. Retrieved from https://www.forbes.com/sites/niallmccarthy/2017/06/20/which-countries-have-the-highest-levels-of-labor-union-membership-infographic/?sh=176fcbe733c0. Accessed on February 14, 2020.

5. Bruenig, M. (2018, November 08). *Public wealth in the US and Nordic countries*. Retrieved from https://www.peoplespolicyproject.org/2018/11/08/public-wealth-in-the-us-and-nordic-countries/. Accessed on February 14, 2020.

CHAPTER 3

1. What is Automation? - ISA. (n.d.). Retrieved from https://www.isa.org/about-isa/what-is-automation/. Accessed on February 12, 2020.

2. Robotics Online Marketing Team. (2017, January 1). *The history of robotics in the automotive industry.* Retrieved from https://www.robotics.org/blog-article.cfm/The-History-of-Robotics-in-the-Automotive-Industry/24. Accessed on March 3, 2020.

3. Anyoha, R. (2017, August 28). *The history of artificial intelligence.* Retrieved from http://sitn.hms.harvard.edu/flash/2017/history-artificial-intelligence/. Accessed on March 4, 2020.

4. West, D. M. (2019, October 25). *What is artificial intelligence?.* Retrieved from https://www.brookings.edu/research/what-is-artificial-intelligence/. Accessed on March 3, 2020.

5. Ali, M., & Quattrucci, L. (2019, February 19). *Machine learning: What's in it for government?.* Retrieved from https://aws.amazon.com/blogs/machine-learning/machine-learning-whats-in-it-for-government/. Accessed on March 3, 2020.

6. Lardieri, A. (2019, June 26). *Robots will replace 20 million jobs by 2030, oxford report finds.* Retrieved from https://www.usnews.com/news/economy/articles/2019-06-26/report-robots-will-replace-20-million-manufacturing-jobs-by-2030. Accessed on March 4, 2020.

7. Tilley, J. (2017, September 7). *Automation, robotics, and the factory of the future.* Retrieved from https://www.mckinsey.com/business-functions/operations/our-insights/automation-robotics-and-the-factory-of-the-future. Accessed on March 9, 2020.

8. Associated Press. (2019, January 24). *Over 30 million U.S. workers will lose their jobs because of AI.* Retrieved from https://www.marketwatch.com/story/ai-is-set-to-replace-36-million-us-workers-2019-01-24

9. Juniper Research: Retailer Spending on AI to Grow Nearly Fourfold, Reaching $7.3 Billion by 2022. (2018, January 31). Retrieved from https://www.businesswire.com/news/home/20180131005068/en/Juniper-Research-Retailer-Spending-AI-Grow-Fourfold. Accessed on March 10, 2020.

10. Collier, M., Fu, R., Yin, L., & Christiansen, P. (2017). *Artificial intelligence: Healthcare's new nervous system.* Retrieved from https://www.accenture.com/t20171215 T032059Z__w__/us-en/_acnmedia/PDF-49/Accenture-Health-Artificial-Intelligence.pdf#zoom=50. Accessed on February 21, 2020.

11. Lund, S., Manyika, J., Segel, L. H., Dua, A., Hancock, B., Rutherford, S., & Macon, B. (2019, November 07). *The future of work in America: People and places, today and tomorrow.* Retrieved from https://www.mckinsey.com/featured-insights/future-of-work/the-future-of-work-in-america-people-and-places-today-and-tomorrow. Accessed on February 27, 2020.

12. Moran, G. (2020, January 14). *Your job will be automated-here's how to figure out when A.I. could take over.* Retrieved from https://fortune.com/2019/08/01/predicting-job-automation-ai/. Accessed on February 17, 2020.

13. Forrester. (n.d.). *The future of work.* Retrieved from https://go.forrester.com/future-of-work/?utm_source=forrester_news&utm_medium=web&utm_campaign=futureofwork. Accessed on March 14, 2020.

14. Talty, S. (2018, April). *What will our society look like when artificial intelligence is everywhere?.* Retrieved from https://www.smithsonianmag.com/innovation/artificial-intelligence-future-scenarios-180968403/. Accessed on March 17, 2020.

15. Stanford University HAI. (2019). *AI Index 2019.* Retrieved from https://hai.stanford.edu/research/ai-index-2019. Accessed on March 17, 2020.

16. Mills, T. (2018, August 29). *Council post: how far are we from truly human-like AI?.* Retrieved from https://www.forbes.com/sites/forbestechcouncil/2018/08/28/how-far-are-we-from-truly-human-like-ai/#44a6ab8031ac. Accessed on February 22, 2020.

17. Hoban, B. (2018, May 23). *Artificial intelligence will disrupt the future of work. Are we ready?.* Retrieved from https://www.brookings.edu/blog/brookings-now/2018/05/23/artificial-intelligence-will-disrupt-the-future-of-work-are-we-ready/. Accessed on February 22, 2020.

CHAPTER 4

1. Google. (n.d.). *About Google, our culture & company news*. Retrieved from https://about.google/. Accessed on January 15, 2020.
2. University of Houston. (2010). *HoustonPBS: The channel that changes you*. Retrieved from https://web.archive.org/web/20110511081424/http://www.houstonpbs.org/site/PageServer?pagename=abt_history. Accessed on March 18, 2020.
3. Florida National University. (2019, August 15). *The evolution of distance learning*. Retrieved from https://www.fnu.edu/evolution-distance-learning/. Accessed on March 18, 2020.
4. United States Army Human Resources Command. (n.d.). *Correspondence courses*. Retrieved from https://www.hrc.army.mil/content/Army Correspondence Course Program ACCP. Accessed on February 22, 2020.
5. McGovern, S. L., Gill, S., Myers, C., & Gera, M. (2018). *The new age: Artificial intelligence for human resource opportunities and functions*. Retrieved from https://hrlens.org/wp-content/uploads/2019/11/EY-the-new-age-artificial-intelligence-for-human-resource-opportunities-and-functions.pdf. Accessed on March 12, 2020.
6. Heilweil, R. (2019, December 12). *Artificial intelligence will help determine if you get your next job*. Retrieved from https://www.vox.com/recode/2019/12/12/20993665/artificial-intelligence-ai-job-screen. Accessed on February 1, 2020.
7. Harwell, D. (2019, November 06). *A face-scanning algorithm increasingly decides whether you deserve the job*. Retrieved from https://www.washingtonpost.com/technology/2019/10/22/ai-hiring-face-scanning-algorithm-increasingly-decides-whether-you-deserve-job/. Accessed on February 1, 2020.
8. Vidal, E. (2020, July 24). *The role of artificial intelligence in the hiring process*. Retrieved from https://talentculture.com/the-role-of-artificial-intelligence-in-the-hiring-process/. Accessed on February 1, 2020.
9. Feloni, R. (2017, June 28). *Consumer-goods giant unilever has been hiring employees using brain games and artificial intelligence – and it's a huge success*. Retrieved from https://www.businessinsider.com/unilever-artificial-intelligence-hiring-process-2017-6. Accessed on February 1, 2020.

10. Romeo, J. (2020, February 28). *Artificial intelligence boosts employee performance*. Retrieved from https://www.shrm.org/resourcesandtools/hr-topics/technology/pages/artificial-intelligence-boosts-employee-performance.aspx. Accessed on March 25, 2020.

11. Buck, B., & Morrow, J. (2018). AI, performance management and engagement: Keeping your best their best. *Strategic HR Review, 17(5)*, 261–262. doi:10.1108/shr-10-2018-145

12. Marr, B. (2017, January 17). *The future of performance management: How AI and big data combat workplace bias*. Retrieved from https://www.forbes.com/sites/bernardmarr/2017/01/17/the-future-of-performance-management-how-ai-and-big-data-combat-workplace-bias/#2787d2bf4a0d. Accessed on March 22, 2020.

13. Sammer, J. (2020, February 28). *Bringing artificial intelligence into pay decisions*. Retrieved from https://www.shrm.org/resourcesandtools/hr-topics/compensation/pages/bringing-artificial-intelligence-into-pay-decisions.aspx. Accessed on March 22, 2020.

14. Barnard, D. (2019, August 16). *Examples of how AI is transforming learning and development*. Retrieved from https://virtualspeech.com/blog/ai-ml-learning-development. Accessed on March 29, 2020.

15. The Nukon Team. (2019, October 24). *AI for workplace safety: How does it fit?*. Retrieved from https://www.nukon.com/blog/ai-for-workplace-safety-how-does-it-fit. Accessed on March 30, 2020.

16. EHS Insight Resources. (2019, August 28). *AI workplace safety: What you need to know*. Retrieved from https://www.ehsinsight.com/blog/ai-workplace-safety-what-you-need-to-know. Accessed on March 31, 2020.

CHAPTER 5

1. Columbus, L. (2018, August 16). *IoT market predicted to double by 2021, reaching $520B*. Retrieved from https://www.forbes.com/sites/louiscolumbus/2018/08/16/iot-market-predicted-to-double-by-2021-reaching-520b/#5fa959541f94. Accessed on June 1, 2020.

2.   Lund, S., Manyika, J., Segel, L. H., Dua, A., Hancock, B.,
      Rutherford, S., & Macon, B. (2019, November 07). *The
      future of work in America: People and places, today and
      tomorrow*. Retrieved from https://www.mckinsey.com/
      featured-insights/future-of-work/the-future-of-work-in-
      america-people-and-places-today-and-tomorrow. Accessed
      on February 27, 2020.
3.   Kelly, J. (2019, September 30). *Unbridled adoption of
      artificial intelligence may result in millions of job losses and
      require massive retraining for those impacted*. Retrieved
      from   https://www.forbes.com/sites/jackkelly/2019/09/30/
      unbridled-adoption-of-artificial-intelligence-may-result-in-
      millions-of-job-losses-and-require-massive-retraining-for-
      those-impacted/#e06778d1de78. Accessed on May 11,
      2020.
4.   Frey, C. (2019, April 01). *Will AI destroy more jobs than it
      creates over the next decade?*. Retrieved from https://
      www.wsj.com/articles/will-ai-destroy-more-jobs-than-it-
      creates-over-the-next-decade-11554156299. Accessed on
      June 20, 2020.
5.   Klemmer, K. (2009). Job openings and hires decline in
      2008. *Monthly Labor Review*, (May), 32–44. Retrieved
      from https://www.bls.gov/opub/mlr/2009/05/art2full.pdf
6.   Turczynski, B. (2021, January 04). *2021 HR statistics: Job
      search, hiring, recruiting & interviews*. Retrieved from
      https://zety.com/blog/hr-statistics. Accessed on January 12,
      2021.

CHAPTER 6

1.   El Mahgiub, M. (Director). (2019). *Education: Preparing
      students for jobs that don't yet exist* [Video file]. Spain:
      TEDx Talks. Retrieved from https://www.youtube.com/
      watch?v=uGR4eJmNI90. Accessed on November 24,
      2020.
2.   Neelakantan, S. (2020, November 04). *Successful AI
      examples in higher education that can inspire our
      future*. Retrieved from https://edtechmagazine.com/
      higher/article/2020/01/successful-ai-examples-higher-edu-
      cation-can-inspire-our-future. Accessed on July 7, 2020.

3. German Center for Research and Innovation. (n.d.). *AI research takes root in Germany.* Retrieved from https://www.dwih-newyork.org/en/current-focus-topics/artificial-intelligence/ai-research-takes-root-in-germany/. Accessed on July 8, 2020.

4. Haas, B. (2018, April 05). *'Killer robots': AI experts call for boycott over lab at South Korea University.* Retrieved from https://www.theguardian.com/technology/2018/apr/05/killer-robots-south-korea-university-boycott-artifical-intelligence-hanwha. Accessed on July 11, 2020.

5. @iLabAfrica. (n.d.). *@iLabAfrica – @iBizAfrica incubation and innovation centre.* Retrieved from http://www.ilabafrica.ac.ke/index.php/ibizafrica/. Accessed on July 1, 2020.

6. Microsoft News Center. (2020, April 28). *University of Sydney builds AI-infused corona chatbot to support students with COVID-19 queries.* Retrieved from https://news.microsoft.com/en-au/features/university-of-sydney-builds-ai-infused-corona-chatbot-to-support-students-with-covid-19-queries/. Accessed on June 30, 2020.

7. Hanno, E. S., Nason, E., Taska, B., Bakthavachalam, V., Glassberg Sands, E., Bowley, R., ... Keveloh, K. (2020, January). *Jobs of tomorrow mapping opportunity in the new economy.* Retrieved from http://www3.weforum.org/docs/WEF_Jobs_of_Tomorrow_2020.pdf. Accessed on June 27, 2020.

CHAPTER 8

1. The World Bank. (2020, June 21). *Labor force, total.* Retrieved from https://data.worldbank.org/indicator/SL.TLF.TOTL.IN. Accessed on January 12, 2021.

2. Vollset, S., Goren, E., Yuan, C., Cao, J., Smith, A. E., Hsiao, T., ... Murray, C. J. L. (2020). Fertility, mortality, migration, and population scenarios for 195 countries and territories from 2017 to 2100: A forecasting analysis for the Global Burden of Disease Study. *Lancet, 396,* 1285–1306. doi:10.1016/S0140-6736(20)30677-2

3. The World Bank. (2020, September 20). *Unemployment, total (% of total labor force) (modeled ILO estimate).* Retrieved from https://data.worldbank.org/indicator/SL.UEM.TOTL.ZS. Accessed on January 12, 2021.

4.   Walinga, J., & Stanger, C. (2010). 12.3 Is personality more nature or more nurture? Behavioral and molecular genetics. In *Introduction to Psychology: 1st Canadian Edition*. BCcampus. Retrieved from https://opentextbc.ca/introductiontopsychology/chapter/11-3-is-personality-more-nature-or-more-nurture-behavioral-and-molecular-genetics/. Accessed on April 13, 2021.

5.   Perry, E. M. (2019). *What does passing on values to the next generation really look like?* (Wealth of Wisdom: The Top 50 Questions Wealthy Families Ask) (T. McCullough & K. Whitaker, Eds.). Chichester: John Wiley & Sons, pp. 23–30.

CHAPTER 9

1.   Radu, S. (2019, August 19). *Despite China's efforts, the U.S. still leads in artificial intelligence*. Retrieved from https://www.usnews.com/news/best-countries/articles/2019-08-19/the-us-is-still-the-global-leader-in-artificial-intelligence. Accessed on July 7, 2020.

2.   Stanford University HAI. (2019). *Global AI vibrancy tool*. Retrieved from https://vibrancy.aiindex.org/. Accessed on August 8, 2020.

3.   Oxford Insights. (2019). *Government AI readiness index 2019 – Oxford insights*. Retrieved from https://www.oxfordinsights.com/ai-readiness2019. Accessed on August 8, 2020.

4.   National Geographic Society. (2019, December 09). *Industrial revolution and technology*. Retrieved from https://www.nationalgeographic.org/article/industrial-revolution-and-technology/. Accessed on September 10, 2020.

5.   Shierholz, H. (2020, January 22). *The number of workers represented by a union held steady in 2019, while union membership fell*. Retrieved from https://www.epi.org/publication/2019-union-membership-data/. Accessed on September 8, 2020.

6.   McCarthy, N., & Richter, F. (2019, May 07). *Infographic: the state of global trade union membership*. Retrieved from https://www.statista.com/chart/9919/the-state-of-the-unions/. Accessed on September 10, 2020.

7. Zhang, J. (2017). The evolution of China's one-child policy and its effects on family outcomes. *Journal of Economic Perspectives, 31*(1), 141–160.

8. Chelala, C. (2016, May 14). *The plight of China's "left behind" children.* Retrieved from https://www.theglobalist.com/the-plight-of-chinas-left-behind-children/. Accessed on September 12, 2020.

9. Kearney, A. T. (2017, September 18). *A. T. Kearney 2017 global services location index spotlights automation as massive job displacer.* Retrieved from https://www.multivu.com/players/English/8179851-at-kearney-2017-global-services-location-index/. Accessed on October 30, 2020.

CHAPTER 10

1. Bohrer, B. (2019, June 28). *Alaska governor slashes university budget by $130 million.* Retrieved from https://www.seattletimes.com/seattle-news/northwest/dunleavy-slashes-university-budget-by-130-million/. Accessed on November 24, 2020.

2. Samuel, S. (2020, February 19). *Everywhere basic income has been tried, in one map.* Retrieved from https://www.vox.com/future-perfect/2020/2/19/21112570/universal-basic-income-ubi-map. Accessed on November 24, 2020.

3. Adamczyk, A. (2020, June 25). *People receiving unemployment benefits are actually more likely to look for jobs, new study finds.* Retrieved from https://www.cnbc.com/2020/06/25/people-receiving-unemployment-benefits-are-more-likely-to-look-for-jobs.html. Accessed on November 24, 2020.

4. Freedom Dividend. (2019, December 01). *How we'll pay for the freedom dividend.* Retrieved from https://freedomdividend.com/. Accessed on November 24, 2020.

5. Christiano, L. J. (2017, February 7). *The great recession: A macroeconomic earthquake.* Retrieved from https://www.minneapolisfed.org/article/2017/the-great-recession-a-macroeconomic-earthquake. Accessed on November 24, 2020.

6. Sasagawa, M., Amieux, P. S., & Martzen, M. R. (2017). Health equity and the gini index in the United States. *Health Equity and the Gini Index in the United States*, 2(2), 1–4.

7. Index Mundi. (2020, November 27). *Denmark GDP – Composition by sector*. Retrieved from https://www.in-dexmundi.com/denmark/gdp_composition_by_sector.html. Accessed on January 12, 2021.

8. Amabile, T. M., Barsade, S. G., Mueller, J. S., & Staw, B. M. (2005). Affect and creativity at work. *Administrative Science Quarterly*, 50(3), 367–403.

INDEX